Green Wood Chairs

Green Wood Chairs

Chairs and chairmakers of Ireland

Alison Ospina (signature)

Alison Ospina

Stobart Davies

British Library Cataloguing in Publication Data.

A catalogue record of this book is available from the British Library.

ISBN 978-0-85442-151-0

Published 2009 by
Stobart Davies Limited
Stobart House, Pontyclerc,
Penybanc Road, Ammanford,
Carmarthenshire SA18 3HP, UK
www.stobartdavies.com

Layout and design Stobart Davies Ltd

Cover photo taken by Roland Paschhoff at the Faerie Fort, Rosscarbery, West Cork

Photography by Ben Russell and Roland Paschhoff

Drawings by Mike Prankerd

Printed in Glasgow by Bell & Bain Ltd

photograph page 2: if you go down to the woods today
photograph page 6: detail mortice and tenon joint hazel

Contents

For my father and for Jose,
Ana, Eddy and Rosa

Introduction

Introduction

*Joyful exaltation in perfection of craft as art
and the perfection of self.*
The Way of the Carpenter
William Coaldrake

Making chairs makes people smile

This book is as much about trees as it is about chairs. Without the material, energy and inspiration of trees, my chairs would never have been born. Like the woodland, a green wood chair maker's life develops a rhythm according to the seasons. Winter months are spent gathering hazel and inspiration for next year's creations. Designs for my chairs take seed during the long, cold, winter months, when the bare branches show stark against the winter sky. The designs develop with no conscious intent, the negative spaces created by the twisting branches get under my skin and into my brain. I cannot simply look at a tree without seeing those shapes. The spring and summer months are spent putting that inspiration into action, when the spiritual and the material combine artistically and become, in my case, chairs.

The pleasure of going with the flow

All the processes of green wood chair making are a joy; there is not one part of the job that doesn't feel good. It is fun to see the curly, bark-edged peelings that spin from the tenoner or to sit quietly outside removing ribbons of bark. Green wood chair making challenges you to be intuitive and to trust your intuition. Unlike joinery, it is not to do with getting it square or measuring in millimetres, rather it is feeling if something is

opposite: coming home
left: inside Green Wood Chairs studio

9

My second attempt

right and judging the angle by eye and selecting the sticks. These are unquantifiable processes that are neither right nor wrong. It is simple without being easy.

I use 'ish' a lot in instructions. The sticks should be straight-ish, the measurement should be three-ish. This is not because this is sloppy, careless woodwork but because we are not really working from a plan. For example, we set out to make a child's chair, we might decide that the back posts should measure 20" but if they end up measuring 21" or 22", it does not matter as we let the materials decide. If the stick has an interesting knobbly bit, include it, if it suddenly bends in the wrong direction, cut it slightly shorter. Relinquish the control you normally have over your materials. You are working with the wood and not imposing a form upon it.

There are certain things that must be accurate but that accuracy is measured by eye and you develop that accuracy through experience. You learn to trust that you know much more than you ever thought you knew. For example, when I say, 'make sure it is sitting flat' you may think, 'how do I do that?' If I say, 'just make sure it is sitting flat' and then you do it, you realise you knew this all along. However, if something goes seriously wrong, it was not meant to be. Put the stick in the fire and choose another one.

My journey

I started making green wood chairs when I moved to West Cork in 1996. I was inspired by the magic of the landscape and wanted to create my own work. I had seen a stick chair in a book and was intrigued by the idea. Coincidentally, a friend gave me some hazel sticks and still rather uncertain, I decided to have a go. I made my first chair the very day the

In Chinese philosophy, all life systems need a balance. This is known as Tao energy or the Way. Tao runs through everything: culture, philosophy, political systems and living organisms. Reality is a process of continuous flow and change; the two poles that set the limits for these cycles of change are **Yin and Yang**. We need a balance of both to be healthy, successful, effective, creative and loving. **Yang** (associated with the masculine) is rational, competitive, analytic, aggressive and intellectual. In wood work terms this is square, hard edged, accurate measurements, predictable outcomes and so on. **Yin** (associated with the feminine) is responsive, cooperative, intuitive and synthesising. In wood work terms this is soft-edged, free flowing, working with the grain, measuring by eye, allowing materials to dictate.

We all have elements of **Ying and Yang** and in Western thinking they have been referred to as the rational and the intuitive and are complementary functions of the mind. **Green wood work is the Yin to the Yang of joinery, carpentry and cabinet making.** This is the art of the possible where your design ideas are only limited by your ability to carry them out. Once you have developed some skill in the techniques and processes, you apply them automatically or subconsciously, using your body and your intuition to measure and make (rule of thumb). You are working with a yielding material, creating soft flowing forms and working with the grain.

hazel sticks were delivered and knew at that moment that this could become a serious obsession.

Over the following months I made one chair after another. They were not especially good although they had a certain primitive charm. It took me a while to get the proportions right so that the chairs were actually comfortable and functional. I experimented with the thickness of the components. How strong was a 18 mm (¾ in) tenon? How thin could a stretcher be while retaining its strength?

Selecting the materials is hugely important and I was fascinated by the way the chairs seem to build themselves when you select the *right* sticks. A chair made with sticks is a bit like the human face in that you can make the same design, to the same dimensions and still every chair looks slightly different. A bend here, a knobbly bit there, a twist of a foot, all these give the chair character and an animated quality.

Over the years, I have taught all types of people to make chairs. An interesting observation is that each chair, in some way, is like the person who made it. I have helped people to create neat, carefully made chairs, wild, slightly uncomfortable but beautiful chairs, even a chair that grew

above: whittling tenons
left: birch and oak chair
with cherry seat

11

so tall it would not fit into a car when it was time to leave. I have come to realise, to my surprise, that there is at least one chair in everybody!

As well as being pleasing to the eye, there is a real sense of pleasure and pride in using a chair that you have made yourself. You carefully selected, peeled, sanded and polished it and every time you sit down you cannot help exploring with your hands every bump and dip and relishing the feel and shape of the wood.

Different chairs suit different purposes in our houses. In using natural branch wood we can create dining chairs for sitting up at the table, low, comfortable, armchairs for relaxing in and even chairs that are more sculptural than functional, that we just like to gaze at and enjoy. You never feel lonely in a room of green wood chairs as they have an almost animated quality. Each one seems to have a different character, reflecting the grace and beauty of the trees they came from.

right: hazel stool with elm seat
far right: hazel chair with
súgán (oat straw rope) seat
page 14: hazel baby chair
with súgán seat

Chapter 1

Design influences

1. Design influences

Have nothing in your house that you do not know to be useful or believe to be beautiful
William Morris

The first step in designing a chair is a walk in the woods. The story has started here in the colouration of the bark, the shape of the sticks, the way the trees have grown. This is due to the conditions of light, protection from the elements, water availability, prevailing wind and elements in the soil. When you enter the woodland to look for suitable material, you may find you 'can't see the wood for the trees.' The initial search can take a long time, but when you cut your first stem, you wonder why you could not see the obvious profusion all around you. Gradually your eye will spot the stems you want, usually from some way off. By standing back and seeing, the stems stand out from the others, almost shining. This experience is somewhat like a hunter searching in dense woodland for quarry. You develop a 'hunter's eye' that sees things in a way that others cannot see.

You will want the designs to retain the tree's animated energy, to incorporate different stories for each component. Was the wood dense? Was it wet? Was there iron in the soil? Was there plentiful light? Did the

far left: Shaker Rocking Chair, Waterlivet, Ohio Shaker Community, maple with tape seat. Art Complex Museum, Duxbury, Massachusettes
left: Negative spaces – my inspiration

saplings have to grow very tall and straight to find a gap in the canopy? Did animals scratch and chew at the bark and did honeysuckle twist around the tree, biting deep, symmetrical spirals along the branches?

Your work will be to release the energy, to carefully select and to create chairs from this versatile material, often without really knowing what the finished chair will look like. This element of risk is part of the fun as it will challenge you to hone your skills, to make good decisions and to work in an open and intuitive way. Design happens dynamically, each chair is the result of collaboration between materials and maker. These chairs are communicative and friendly, they are tactile and compel you to reach out and touch them. They seem to communicate with people and also with each other. In fact, sharing a room with green wood chairs feels like being amongst old friends. They make you smile.

I am drawn to the Shaker aesthetic. Any genuine Shaker piece is recognisable through the following criteria:

Design
Clean lines, perfect proportion, uncluttered, light, strong and functional.

Material
Carefully selected beautiful, figured hard woods.

Craftsmanship
Excellent making skills, no short cuts, traditional, well-made joints.

The Shakers were not averse to using modern technology and are reputed to have invented a table saw and planer. They produced hundreds of chairs for sale as well as for use in their own communities. Each community produced slightly different designs.

On the other side of the Atlantic, Irish chair making was developing quite differently. There was no Industrial Revolution in Ireland, only famine and grinding poverty for a large part of the population. Furniture in England and Europe was extremely sophisticated and ornately designed but in Ireland furniture was made in a style that was born of necessity, craftsmen were forced to use their ingenuity to make the most of the few materials and tools they possessed.

Many of the remaining chairs dating back to 18th century are known as hedge chairs.

According to some sources, these chairs were not made by professional carpenters but by self-styled hedge carpenters. These were craftsmen who were considered the lowliest of skilled wood workers, often utilising the natural shapes of the branch wood to make chair components, thus saving themselves time and labour. Hedge chairs were made using slab and stick design. These typically have a large D-shaped plank or slab for a seat which can be up to 2″ (50mm) thick with legs and back spindles tenoned and wedged into the plank. The legs are at an angle, with upright spindles and a natural curved branch for the top rail.

Hedge Chair
National Museum of Ireland

There were many practical advantages to making chairs this way. The joints were strong and did not require glue, legs could be changed if damaged, the plank could be of use for generations. It was a style that allowed for variation, depending on the skills and taste of the maker and the materials and tools available.

In the more prosperous parts of Ireland, there was some small-scale production of manufactured chairs. From the 18th to the 20th century, post and rail chairs were made with súgán seating. Súgán (pronounced 'sue gawn') is a type of oat straw rope used on farms and produced in the home. Older members of the community still remember helping with the production of súgán. It provided ideal seating material, warm, comfortable, long lasting, locally available and easily replaced. The frames of súgán chairs were made using post and rail construction, the legs joined by stretchers and rails, tenons pushed through round mortices and secured by wedges and (in some cases) by pegs. Ash was often used for making chair frames, sometimes unseasoned as it is a strong, abundant and easily worked wood which still grows in profusion in many areas of the country.

In certain parts of Ireland, vernacular styles developed, demonstrating ingenious ways of making chairs to fulfil all needs. For example, three-legged chair are best for uneven floors. Large planks were hard to come by, so joining legs to solid planks was done with wedged joints that did not require glue, allowing for the legs to be replaced easily. In Sligo, and later in Tuam, a robust, three-legged chair was designed with a seat that was made up from several small planks. It had a single, wide board up the back and it was almost triangular in shape, with a T-shaped stretcher joining the legs. A version of this chair is still in production today in Tuam.

Looking at the wide variety of chairs made over the last 300 years, it is clear that chair makers of the past, working with limited resources,

right: Súgán Chair
National Museum of Ireland
page 22: Rosa with baby chairs,
in the woods

The Shakers
Hands to Work, Hearts to God

Before I began green wood chair making, I was deeply obsessed with Shaker design. Shakerism can be traced back to 18th century France where a group of persecuted Protestants known as the Camisards fled to England. They worshiped God by dancing, singing, shaking and shouting. This alienated them from the mainstream church as well as the general public. In England, they had been joined by a young woman named Ann Lee who had experienced religious manifestations throughout her life. She became their spiritual leader, and was known as Mother Ann. Continued persecution in England led the Shakers to the United States. Many Americans felt that organised religion was failing to deliver a strong spiritual and moral message and Shakerism brought them hope and moral certainty. Due to the lack of tolerance of their form of worship and way of life, the Shakers began to establish communities that would allow them to live apart from the world.

Shaker orthodoxy called for celibacy, common property holdings, equality of the sexes and pacifism. Believers aimed to lead a blameless life, their principles being purity of mind and body, honesty, integrity, plainness, simplicity, hard work and kindness. They sought harmony between their spiritual and physical environments, a philosophy that led them to create a design aesthetic that has endured long after the Shaker communities have disappeared. Mother Ann held strong views on household possessions, many of which she thought were superfluous to daily life. Her preachings implied that unnecessary and ostentatious surroundings opened the heart to vanity and corrupted the natural materials and purpose of the piece itself.

derived fulfilment and pleasure from creating items that were not just functional but were imbued with the wit and artistry of their maker. In the remaining examples of their work we recognise independent, creative and unpretentious designs that relied on the use of hand tools and traditional skills.

Chapter 2

Hazel
Traditional uses coppicing and magic

2. Hazel — traditional uses, coppicing and magic

I went out to the hazel wood,
Because a fire was in my head,
And cut and peeled a hazel wand,
And hooked a berry to a thread:
And when white moths were on the wing,
And moth-like stars were flickering out,
I dropped the berry in a stream
And caught a little silver trout.
The Song of Wandering Aengus
W.E. Yeats

Humanity is dependent on trees for its survival. Ireland used to be covered in dense oak woods but these days trees are felled and cleared at such a rate that very little forest or woodland remains.

Wood is one of the most important natural materials known to man. It has strength, beauty, flexibility, variety and versatility. No man-made material even comes close to being as useful or as beautiful. Our hands reach out to touch wood, it lifts our spirits to be surrounded by it and it tugs at our souls. We often hear people say 'I love wood' because they are drawn to it. Have you noticed how we want to reach out and touch the rough and polished surfaces? Those of us living in cities may have minimal contact with trees, plants and animals. We can make up for this lack by getting out into the countryside for a walk or a visit. A hazel wood is a beautiful place to walk in for it calms us and gives us a spiritual topping-up that we often sorely need. Hazel woods remind us that we are just creatures of this earth and bring our attention back from our internal dialogue and day-to-day preoccupations to the outside world that is always there for us to enjoy.

Hazel trees are still common throughout Ireland, Britain and Europe. Often self seeded, they thrive beside streams, rivers and ponds, preferring to stand on well-drained soil, with their roots in the water. Hazel is one of the first trees in spring to come into leaf soon after the pollen-laden catkins appear. Pollination is completed relatively early in the year.

In Ireland, the hazel tree was worshipped and was regarded as the Celtic Tree of Knowledge. Legend has it that nine sacred hazel trees grew around Connla's Well where the Salmon of Wisdom received his gift from the guardians of the well. Each hazel tree dropped a sacred hazel nut into the well where the salmon ate them and became imbued with worldly wisdom. According to Keating's *History of Ireland*, MacColl

opposite: favourite west cork tree
below: hazel bark detail

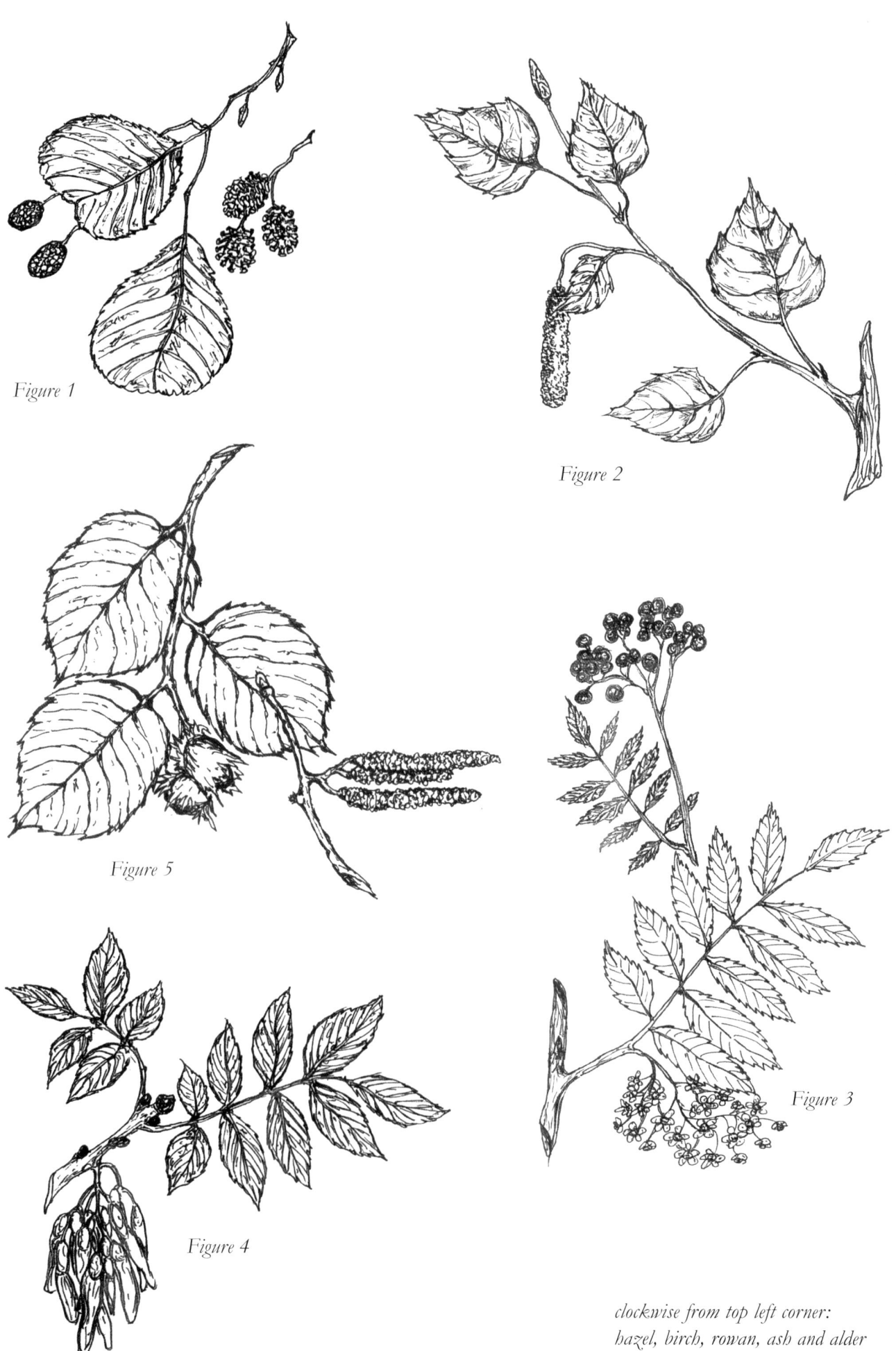

Figure 1

Figure 2

Figure 5

Figure 3

Figure 4

clockwise from top left corner:
hazel, birch, rowan, ash and alder

Hazel side chairs with elm seats, shows how each chairmaker creates something unique, using the same materials.
Alison and Ana Ospina

(meaning son of hazel in Gaelic) was one of the last kings of the mythical Tuatha de Danann. Here the reference to hazel denotes deep wisdom.

The alder is related to the birch and hazel and can be found growing alongside hazel trees on river banks and even in boggy ground. Its bark

Hazel armchair with stool with elm seats (Lissard Estate, West Cork)

is pale grey in colour with lighter greenish patches, making it very attractive for chair making. It is a water-loving tree and is often seen overhanging a stream or river, creating shade for fish and plants. It can be recognised by its round leaves and often shows all four stages of production on the branch at one time: last year's cones, this spring's leaf buds and the male and female catkins. It is the only broadleaf tree to produce cones which often stay on the branch long after fruiting in the autumn. If the bark is damaged, the sap appears with a reddish colour and in ancient times it was thought to bleed. According to Irish legend, the first man was created from alder which was considered a magical tree through which access was gained to the fairy kingdom. Alder was also highly prized for producing the hot-burning charcoal necessary for metal working and the manufacture of weapons.

Birch is a very beautiful, delicate tree which grows well in poor soil and can often been seen at the forest's edge along with alder. It has delicate branches and twigs which, although too fine for chair making, have traditionally been used for besom brooms. However, the lower branches and stems are eminently suitable for chair making. There are thought to be about 60 different species of birch world-wide. Silver birch is a very hardy tree and can survive in the coldest reaches of Northern Europe and Scandinavia. Brown birch can often be found having seeded itself among hazel and other woodland trees. It can be coppiced and produces stems with a dramatic reddish/brown bark and strong, flexible, white wood. Birch, along with hazel, is one of the first trees to leaf in spring and produces pendulous catkins which pollinate the flowers. The female catkin contains hundreds of seeds which are scattered by the wind; it is well known for prolific self -seeding. In ancient times, it was known as the tree of inception and purification and was used in the Celtic Beltaine (May Day) celebrations to light ritual bonfires.

Rowan is a small tree often called mountain ash because it grows at high altitudes and its leaves are very similar to common ash leaves. Rowan blossoms in May, with scented white flowers that give way to small green berries which hang in clusters from the branches. The rowan's clusters of berries turn a dramatic bright red in early autumn, contrasting with the dark green leaves and creating a bold splash of colour in the landscape. You will rarely find an entire woodland of rowan but rather will see it lining city streets or growing amongst other trees, creating diversity often in poor soil and growing conditions. The bark of the rowan is usually grey with very clear horizontal markings. Unlike hazel bark, when rowan dries the bark becomes slightly gnarled but not unattractive. If the bark is stripped off, the revealed wood beneath has a visible grain to it, slightly darker than hazel or birch, light brown rather than white.

Sycamore armchair with elm seat

Rowan is considered to have magical protective influence and was often planted around stone circles and homesteads as a guardian tree. In ancient times, it was used by farmers in spring to deck their cattle sheds, thereby keeping stock and milk safe from evil spirits. In Celtic Ireland, the goddess of spring Brigid was strongly associated with the rowan especially in her role as protector of country folk and their livestock. Brigid was invoked for her influence over spinning and weaving where rowan wood was traditionally used in the making of spindles and spinning wheels. She was later incorporated into Christian mythology and to this day is worshipped as Saint Brigid. In many Irish schools and families the first day of spring (1 February) is still celebrated with a rush woven into a Saint Brigid's cross.

Ancient wisdom guided many practices so that people had an awareness of the energy of the trees that surrounded them which were not simply differentiated by their leaves and fruit. We are no longer guided by that wisdom. Trees are seen as a resource and not as beings which share our planet and can influence our lives. If we open our hearts to their energy, we can rediscover our connection to the vast life force, past and present, that surrounds us. Personally speaking, I feel a kinship with hazel. I have linked myself with the species through ten years of working with it. Without consciously intending to, I have grown aware of its life force or energy. It is a strikingly attractive tree, with multi-coloured varieties of bark. If coppiced with care, it grows in such a way that most branches are usable as chair components. Its main stems are tall with very few side shoots, branching out at the top with interesting forked twigs that are useful as decorative details. The bark strips easily and the wood itself when worked green is yielding and aromatic. It is a pleasure to drill into sappy sticks that emit a smell of roasting hazelnuts!

Alder, birch and rowan (mountain ash) are also suitable for chair making and it is surprising to find that each wood behaves slightly differently. They all have a different smell and you will find that rowan for example has a visible grain. Alder, when stripped of its bark, is a slightly pink colour whereas birch wood is very white but has a magnificent red bark that polishes beautifully and makes very dramatic chairs. There tends to be less waste with hazel because it grows so straight and tall.

'Every species growing in the coppice has its individual character. Some properties are shared — for example you can wind a good withy (rope) from hazel, willow, birch or elm but many are quite singular to a particular species, such as the resilience of ash or the durability of chestnut. Craftsmen match these properties to the specific needs of every product they make, which is why they work so well, and why this wisdom is just as essential today as it was a century or more ago.' Raymond Tabor, *Traditional Woodland Crafts*.

Coppicing is an entirely sustainable way to manage woodland. It has been practised for súgán of years, producing material for fences, tool handles, thatching spars, sheep hurdles, bean rods, hut building, creating tracks, hazelnuts to eat and many other uses we can only guess at. Hazel is also the material of choice for water divining and a wizard's

below: weeping copper beech tree which looks like a triffid!
opposite page: West Cork trees — gnarly ash in winter

staff. It is the commonest and finest coppice wood and has played an important part in rural life for many centuries, if not millennia. Coppicing requires a minimum area of woodland measuring roughly seven acres. Each year one acre is cut and by the time you get to the end, the first acre is ready for cutting again. The wood is grown almost as a crop. The whole tree is cut to a height of just six inches from the ground, when the sap is low and the tree dormant ideally between November and March. During the following growing season, stems will be sent up to a height of around 1.5 metres (4 ft); it recovers very quickly and is invigorated by the extreme pruning. Woodlands managed in this way have been known to last for many hundreds of years.

However, it is not only the products of the woodland that are the reward of coppicing. By managing woodland in this way, there is no need for replanting and each coppice can retain its genetic individuality (which might help to explain why the bark differs in colouration from one woodland to another). We are also maintaining biodiversity, habitats for wild life and ensuring peaceful places for a gentle stroll, enhanced by primroses and bluebells. There have been times when I don't want to cut hazel stems as they seem so perfect where they are. When this happens my advice is to walk away. Some quarry is more valuable left alive for the rest of the world to enjoy.

left: hazel coppice
following page: hazel Side Chair
elm seat (photo taken at Lissard
Estate West Cork)

Chapter 3
Getting your wood

3. Getting your wood

The leaves of the tree are for the healing of the nations
The Book of Revelations

Traditionally, small diameter wood such as hazel is cut into rods (under 40 mm (1½ in) and poles (anything over 40 mm (1½ in)). I rarely use material over 40 mm (1½ in) and I use the term sticks. Throughout this book, all material that has been cut will be referred to as sticks. Material that is not cut is referred to as stems.

Hazel and other suitable woods grow in the hedgerows beside roads, by the river bank and in woodland. If you want to cut wood for chair making, be certain that you are not going to annoy a landowner, local council, park ranger and so forth. It is possible to purchase this kind of material in the UK (see appendix for more details).

In Ireland, there is no known tradition of coppicing although I am certain it would have been practised in ancient times. Ask for hazel, ash and alder when the local council or contractors are clearing trees from electricity cables or from the side of the road. They are often pleased to see the wood going to good use.

In some parts of Ireland, hazel is more easily available than others. There are organisations that can help such as the Irish Coppice Association and Crann which looks after tree planting and woodland protection (further details available in the appendix). It is also worthwhile asking friends and neighbours as well as people who have hazel growing along the borders of their properties. The trees will benefit from the pruning and will grow back again within a few years. The best material to look for comes from trees that have been cut relatively recently, within the last eight to ten years. There will be lots of new growth and it will be fairly straight. When I first started looking for a regular supply of hazel, I was fortunate to be offered by the Irish Forestry Board, Coillte, the opportunity to cut trees along a mile of old railway track. These trees had not been cut for over 50 years but with careful pruning I managed to make over 30 chairs using that hazel. Where there's a will there is definitely a way and once the inspiration grabs you, you can find suitable material almost anywhere.

I recommend a pruning saw for cutting sticks. This is very well suited to cutting between the stems of a hazel tree. It gets into small spaces and is very sharp. I used a bow saw before but found it a bit large and awkward in comparison. Due to its size and shape, the bow saw can only cut from the outside in, whereas the pruning saw is more versatile. Pruning saws are widely available and come in a variety of sizes. It folds away neatly like a pen knife when not in use and is useful at any time of year.

opposite: favourite tree of West Cork – Lissard Estate
below (top): detail pruning saw
below (bottom): pruning saw

Figure 6

If you are coppicing, as opposed to just pruning stems as needed, you will be cutting trees during their dormant phase which is between October/November and February/March, when the trees have no leaves or nuts on them. Cut the entire tree to a height of about 6 inches from the ground. It is important to ensure the stumps have a slight slope to them so that rainwater will run off and the tree stump will not rot.

Once the stems are felled, they can be reduced by taking off the side shoots and twiggy tops. Use your pruning saw for the thicker components and a pair of long handled loppers for the smaller branches and twigs.

top: bill hook
right: cutting hazel stems
with a pruning saw

A bill hook is also suitable if you are lucky enough to have one. These tools are not often seen nowadays, they were commonly used by woodsmen to cut off side branches. Be careful not to damage the bark of the main stem when you are removing the side branches.

Leave the off cuts neatly hidden in the woods where their decomposition will do no harm, nor look untidy and will provide good habitats for insects, birds and general wildlife. Take some straps or ropes with you as you may need to carry your sticks for some distance before packing them into your car or trailer. Sticks are surprisingly heavy and if you can bundle them together they can be more easily dragged or carried. Try to protect the bark as it is easily damaged when the stems are freshly cut.

Cut only as many sticks as you will need for the number of chairs, stools or tables you plan to make in the following six to eight weeks. With experience, you can actually identify at this stage which material is

suitable for back legs, front legs, rails and stretchers, spindles and arms. You want your material to remain green. It is a much more pleasant and yielding material to work with if the sap has not dried out.

Leaving wood to season (dry out) or not is a contentious subject. Many books and practitioners say that you must leave the wood to season before making anything. Many reasons are given: the wood needs to be stable; the joints will shrink and come loose as the chair seasons; the stripped components will crack as they dry and so on. These are all admirably good reasons but from my own experience I know that by using the wood green (even the day it is cut) you gain an advantage. The mortice part of the joint shrinks onto the tenon and is thereby stronger than it would be using dry timber, a snug fit and glue. Also, if you leave the bark on, the wood dries out slowly and does not crack. The bark stays on if it hasn't been damaged, and even the mosses and lichens stay on after the chair had dried out. Occasionally, a component that I have stripped of bark does crack but it is unusual. It could happen if I have stripped a very green component measuring more than 4 cm (1½ in) in diameter and have taken it inside during the winter when the heating is on. However, I will allow that green wood when cut and stripped, may crack, especially if not allowed to dry out slowly enough but there are simple ways of preventing this from happening and they will be detailed in the following chapters.

Once you have brought your sticks home they should be stored in a manner that prevents rot. Any part of the material that is in contact with the earth is at risk of rotting. I store mine leaning up against a bank with their feet on the ground. They normally last like this for several months from February/March to September/October.

The ideal conditions in which to store your wood is an open-sided barn with a roof and no walls. This way the tops and ends are kept dry but the sticks are still out in the elements and will not dry out too quickly. Don't worry if you do not have such facilities. Your sticks are not going to rot straight away after cutting. My advice is to only collect what you truly need and keep it standing up outside if at all possible.

At this stage you are going to be very inspired and excited. You are going to want to start making something immediately and the good news is that you can.

top: long handled loppers detail
opposite page: bundles of coppiced hazel tied with willow withies
following page: curved drawknife

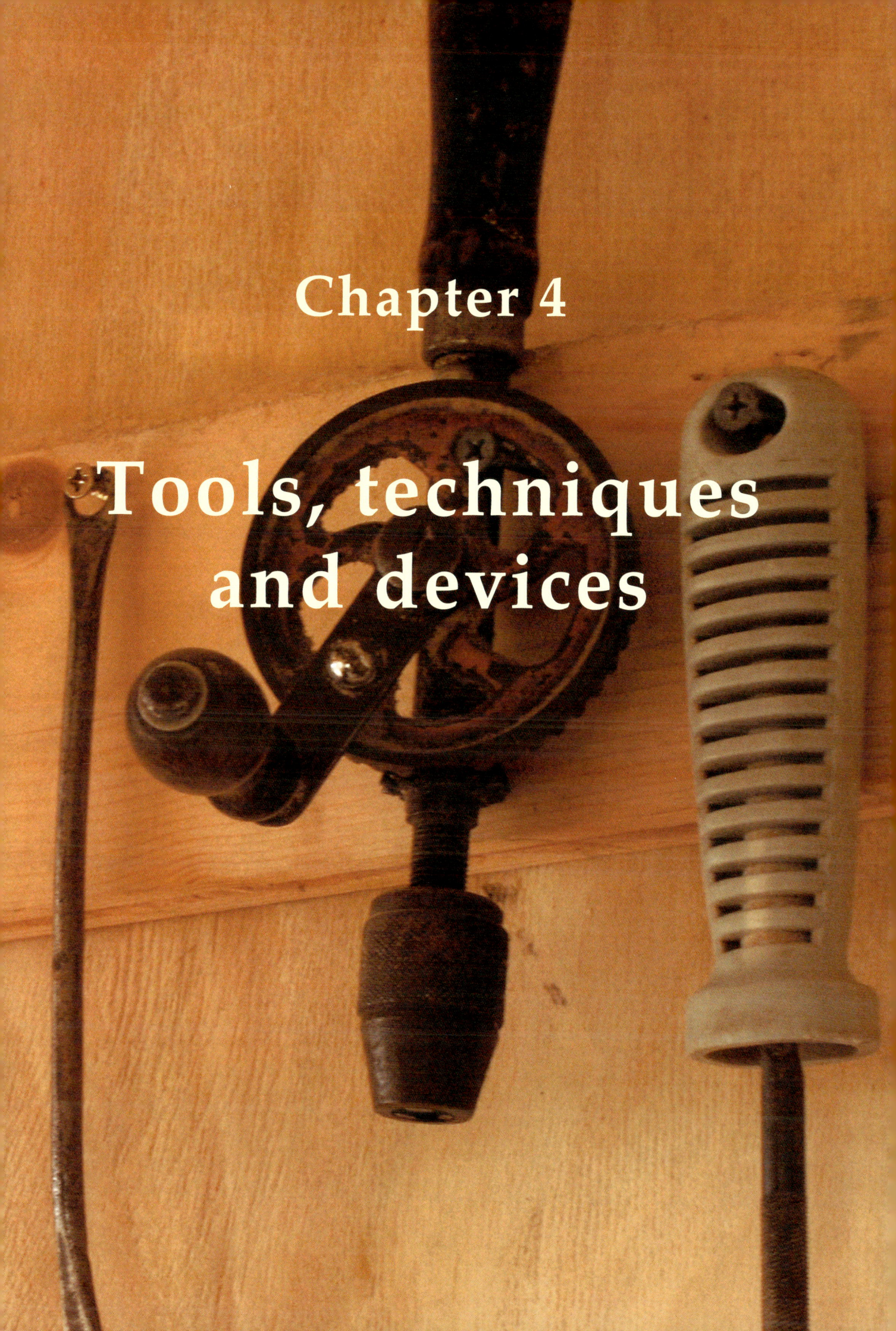

Chapter 4

Tools, techniques and devices

4. Tools, techniques and devices

The tools – the dogu – link the men, the materials and the method
William Coaldrake
The way of the carpenter

Without tools we could not make chairs, they are the link through which our hands connect with our materials. Over time, the tools we use begin to feel familiar to our hands and skills develop simply by repeating the same action. We should keep in mind the Samurai concept that it is the thousandth sword stroke that is perfect – not the first.

The fundamental joint used is the tenon and mortice joint. Put simply, it is a round peg (tenon) on the end of one stick, fitting snugly and deeply into a hole (mortice) drilled in another stick. For a strong joint, the tenon must be slightly longer than it is wide. Never drill the mortice until the tenon is made as the drying out process should happen after the two components are joined. The mortice shrinks onto the tenon and once glued, it makes a joint that is almost impossible to break.

There are various ways of making a tenon. For many years I used a wood turning lathe. I turned the tenons roughly to size, then with my chip carving (whittling) knife and chair maker's gauge I whittled them down to size. They were exactly right when they creaked as I turned them in the hole. I loved this and never realised how time consuming it was.

Nowadays, I make all my tenons with Veritas tenoning attachments. These are fabulous bits of equipment, extremely well made and perfect for the job. They have reduced the time it takes me to make a chair, by half. They work like a giant straight-sided pencil sharpener, attached to a cordless drill.

When making a tenon, always grip the stick in a vice, positioning it as straight as possible. Use the spirit level on the tenoning attachment to

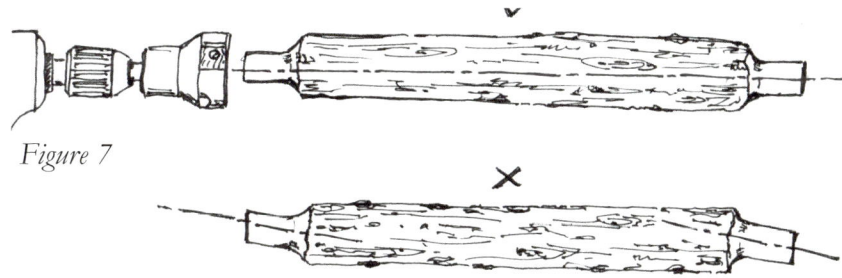

Figure 7

Ensure the tenons are aligned

top left: mortice and tenon components
top right: chairmakers gauges
above left: Veritas tenon cutter in use
above right: holding the drill at
90 degrees to the stick

ensure your tenons line up with each other. This is vital because if the tenons are not in line with each other, the stool or chair you are making will not sit flat on the ground!

Use your drill on the highest torque and speed. Make ¾ inch tenons that are at least 25 mm (1 in) long plus shoulders.

Tenons can also be made (especially in large diameter material) by sawing around the base of the tenon with your stick held sideways in a vice turning it each time you cut. Turn the tenon upright in the vice and chisel down from above. Tidy up with a knife afterwards and it will not have gradually sloping 'shoulders'. For larger pieces such as beds it can be a suitable way to make tenons .

Figures for the measurements of sticks are in both imperial and metric sizes. Veritas tenoning attachments only come in imperial sizes and will be referred to as ¾ in, ⅝ in and 1 in. The multi angle or 3D drill bits only come in metric sizes and will be referred to as 18 mm, 15 mm and 25 mm. Unless otherwise stated, drill bits, when referred to, are always multi angle or 3D bits which are the same thing but named differently by manufacturers.

I used one ¾ inch tenoning attachment for several years but eventually bought the smaller ⅝ inch for spindles and lighter materials. I also invested in a 1 inch tenoner for reducing heavy material down to 18 mm (¾ in). It puts less strain on the drill if you do it in two stages. I use an 18 volt drill on its highest torque and speed settings. There are other tools, both modern and old that can be used for making tenons

Figure 9 — an old pointer or cone cutter used with a traditional carpenter's brace. This tool works on the pencil sharpener principle, leaving the stick with a taper ready to take a tenon cutter. This tool starts the tenon cutting process.

Figure 10 — an old hollow auger also used with a traditional carpenter's brace and in combination with the pointer or cone cutter above. Hollow augers come in different sizes and a variety of designs. If you are lucky you could even find an adjustable hollow auger for sale enabling one cutter to make a range of tenon sizes. They can most often be found in tool sales, jumble sales or vintage tool suppliers.

Figure 11 — A modern steel tenon cutter used in a power drill. These come in a range of sizes for different diameter tenons.

Figures 12 and 13 — Show two modern cutters made in wood. One cuts a starting taper or point and the other the finished tenon. They both work on the pencil sharpener principle and are operated by hand.

Figure 8

above left: tenon square shoulder
above right tenon rounded shoulder

clockwise from top right hand corner:
figure 9 — old pointer/ cone cutter
figure 10 — old fashioned
hollow auger
figure 11 — modern steel
tenon cutter
figure 12 — modern wooden
pointer cutter
figure 13 — modern wooden
tenon cutter
figure 14 — modern tenon cutter
(Ashem crafts)

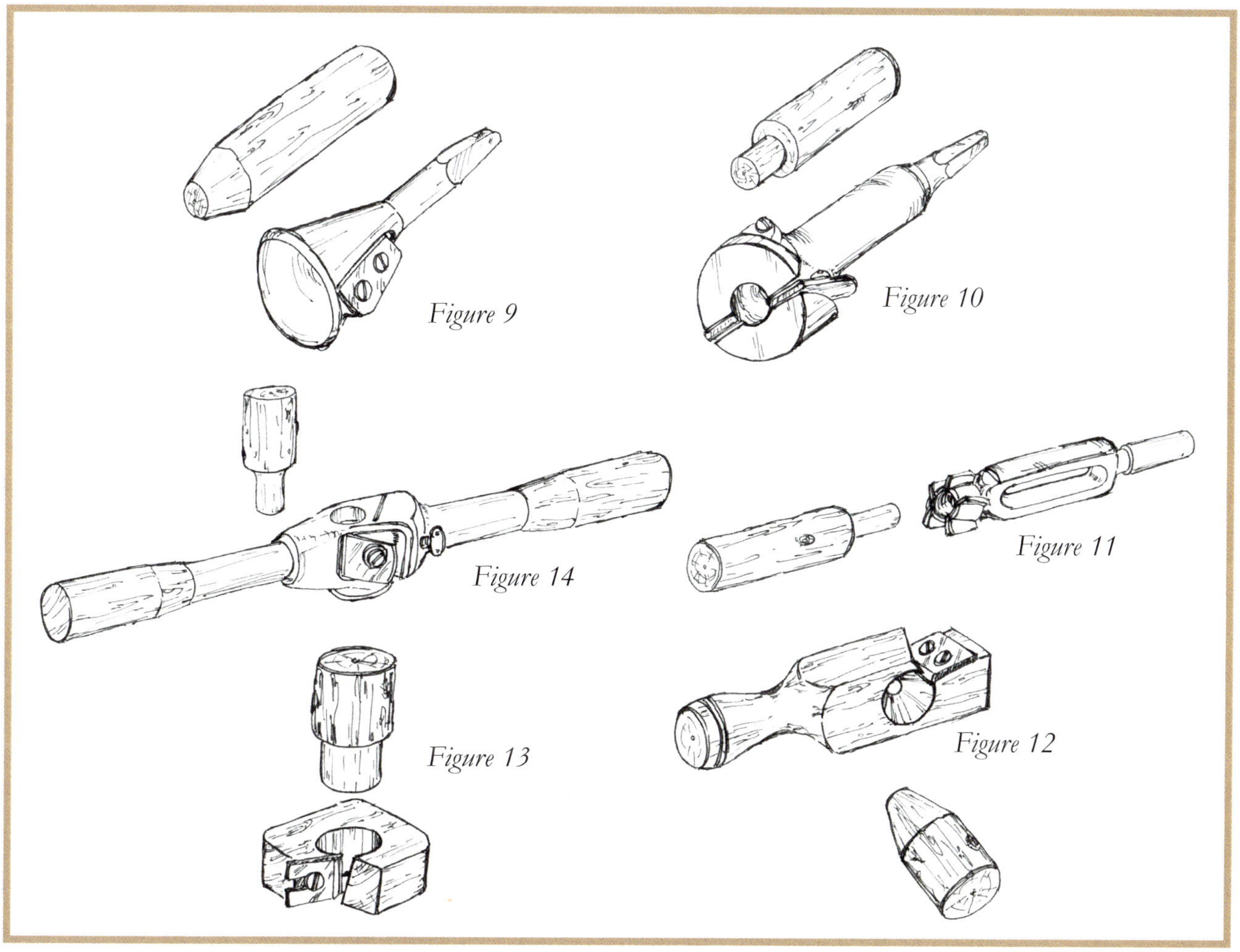

Figure 9

Figure 10

Figure 14

Figure 11

Figure 13

Figure 12

Some chair makers still work with the method used by chair bodgers back in the 18th and 19th centuries. These bodgers spent months in the woods, coppicing and roughly turning the unseasoned chair components on a pole-lathe. A pole lathe is powered by a treadle, attached to a springy sapling. The parts were then stacked up and left to season before being taken to the chair makers who finished the turning and sanding and constructed the chairs.

Shaving horse and drawknife

Figure 14 — A modern tenon cutter made of metal and wood by Ashem Crafts. Available in different sizes for different tenons. It works on the pencil sharpener principle.

Mortices need to be drilled. I use 3D or multi angle drill bits, in combination with either a cordless drill or a pillar drill.

These excellent drill bits are available from good quality tool shops and builders merchants. They are mostly used by carpenters for fitting locks but I like to think they were invented specially for green woodworkers! I have tried using flat (spade) bits but find the point too long. I have also tried Forstner bits but the fibres produced by unseasoned wood tangle themselves around the cutting edges, fill up the gaps and prevent it from cutting. Multi angle drill bits have cut-away sides and the material escapes through the gaps, making them ideal for this job.

Drilling into green wood is not easy on the drill. I really lean into the drill which puts pressure on it but sappy wood is resistant to high speed steel and it can feel a bit like drilling into stone. Some layers drill through easier than others and you get a wonderful aroma of roasting hazelnuts from the heat of the drill bit. An 18 mm drill bit gives the right size hole for a tenon made with a ¾ inch tenoner. A 15 mm drill bit fits the ⅝ in tenoner and the 25mm drill bit fits the 1 in tenoner.

Rounded and flat microplanes

Equipment you need before starting:

- A cordless drill (does not need hammer action but needs two speeds) and high torque 18V
- Whittling (or chip carving) knife
- Sharp cross cutting saw
- White chalk
- PVA woodwork glue
- Bench or workmate
- Multi angle drill bits
- Veritas tenoner (you need ¾ inch or other suitable equipment for making tenons)
- Rubber mallet
- Wooden mallet
- Sharpening stone diamond or stone
- Micro planes
- Plug cutter
- Twist drill bits (various sizes)

Other equipment that is desirable but not essential:

- Pillar drill
- V cradle for holding sticks still for drilling and marking (Figure 6)
- Sash clamps
- Fine toothed Japanese pull saw
- Palm sanders

Take good care of your tools. Put them away clean and dry and do not allow them to lie in the damp or on the ground. Treat them with respect. Spend time sharpening and cleaning them and they will last longer. Replace your knife in its sheath every time you pack up for the day as this way your tools will work better and you will develop an affinity with them. This is one of the pleasures of working with green wood.

Whittling knife and sharpening stone

My favourite knife for general use is a chip carving knife. It has a very short blade and soon begins to feel like an extension of your hand. You will use it for many jobs, stripping, whittling, trimming and so on. You will also need a sharpening stone. This can be an old-fashioned oilstone or, my current favourite, a small, medium-grade, diamond stone used with water. A very sharp edge can be produced quickly and effortlessly using a diamond stone. The only way to learn to sharpen is to keep trying. Hold the knife at a slight angle to the sharpening stone and rub gently with a circular motion. Try it and if it is sharp enough, use it, if not, try again. You will feel a slightly ragged 'burr' on the edge of your knife when it is sharp. I sharpen both sides of my knife, creating a V-shaped edge. If you prefer, create a bevel on just one side of the knife. Do not be afraid to practise and experiment with sharpening.

Techniques

Chair makers gauge (measuring tenons)

To whittle tenons to size, make a gauge from an off cut of seasoned wood, with 15 mm (⅝ in) and 18mm (¾ in)holes. As you whittle, try the tenons in the holes until you have a creaky fit. The sound tells you when

Figure 15

Use a 'V' cradle to hold sticks for drilling

Whittling knife and diamond sharpening stone

Testing the tenon for size

right: whittling the tenon down to size
below: removing bark with
the whittling knife

the tenons are fitting snugly. Hang your gauge on a hook in the workshop as you will need to make regular use of it.

Whittling

Your tenons need to be whittled slightly to make them a good fit. With the ¾ inch tenoner and the 18 mm drill bit the components are almost exactly the same size. Whittling takes the roundness off and leaves gaps in the joint for glue and to let the air escape. However, whittling is one of the most difficult techniques to master. As you are trying to pare away very little material and keep the tenon an even shape, you need to keep careful control of your knife. Hold the stick under your arm, steadying it against the body. I pare lightly and turn the stick after each cut, thereby keeping the tenon round. Keep a chair maker's gauge to hand so that you can try the tenons in the holes.

Bark stripping

When you strip the bark, you will notice that there are three layers: the bark, a pithy layer (this is bright green when the wood is unseasoned) and the wood. Stripping can be done on freshly cut sticks using a chip carving knife. Stand your stick up on the bench or workmate and run the knife down the length of it, taking ribbons of bark as you go. The pithy layer will remain in some places. Use the knife as if you were scraping a carrot to remove the pith. Don't worry about removing every scrap of pith at this stage as you can finish off by sanding later.

A draw knife and a shaving horse is another option. The shaving horse grips the stick, leaving your hands free to use a two handled drawknife.

The shaving horse is simple enough to make yourself and a draw knife can be acquired in many ways.

You may be lucky and find an old draw knife for sale. Perhaps you know a blacksmith who makes tools, or you can buy one from a reputable tool

left: shaving horse
middle: the components of
a shaving horse
below: peeling bark with a
draw knife

Figure 16

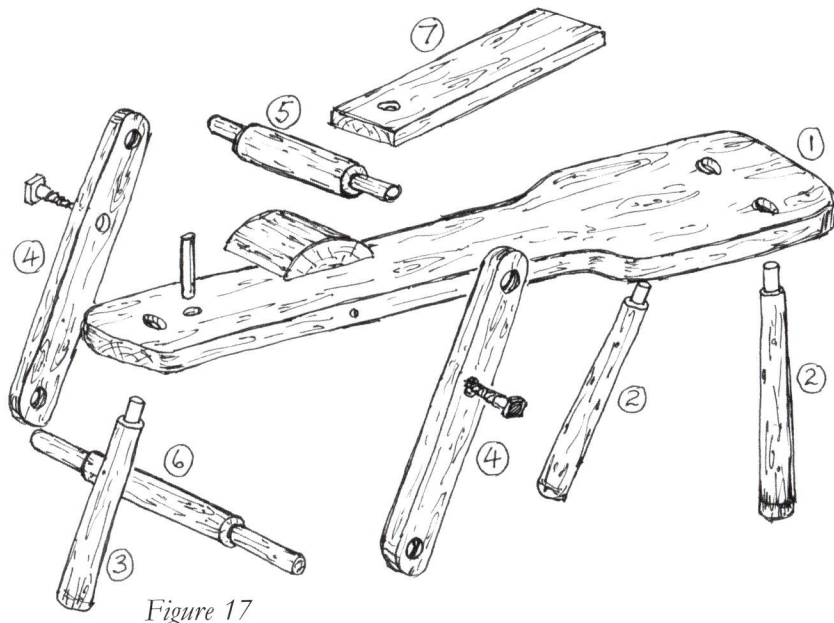

Figure 17

(1) 1530 mm (60 in) long x 300 mm (12 in) wide x 40 mm (1½ in) thick
(2) 460 mm (18 in) long x 40 mm (1½ in) diameter
(3) 400 mm (16 in) long x 40 mm (1½ in) diameter
(4) 660 mm (26 in) long x 100 mm (4 in) wide x 40 mm (1½ in) thick
(5) 380 mm (15 in) long x 80 mm (3 in) diameter
(6) 610 mm (24 in) long x 80 mm (3 in) diameter
(7) 760 mm (30 in) long x 230 mm (9 in) wide x 25 mm (1 in) thick

right: checking depth with a measuring stick
below: marking the centre line with chalk
far right: bundling hazel for transport

supplier (names and addresses in the appendix). I fortunately met a blacksmith just when I needed one. He makes drawknives in a variety of styles out of old Land Rover springs as they are, according to him, made of excellent steel.

Measuring mortice depth

When drilling mortices into small gauge components, you might worry about drilling through the stick and out the other side. A measuring device made from a stripped twig with pencil marks at the appropriate heights will help you to check if you have drilled deeply enough.

Finding the centre point

This is very important and is something you need to check again and again. The centre point of a round stick is its highest point and if you drill off-centre you will have a hole that has one side higher than the other. It is worth intentionally doing it once (on scrap wood) to illustrate the point to yourself.

On a front or back post draw a centre line of white chalk all the way down the stick and mark off the height of the mortices, forming crosses that mark the points to be drilled.

Safety in the woods

Please take the safety of yourself and others into account when gathering hazel sticks. Dress sensibly by wearing strong shoes (preferably with steel toe caps), protective gloves and clothes that will keep the brambles and stinging nettles away. Leather gloves are invaluable when handling branch wood and pulling stems out of the undergrowth. Wear a glove on your left hand (if you are right handed) when sawing or using a bill hook. The hand holding the tool needs a good grip and your bare hand

Safety tip:
Always carry a First Aid kit with you and if possible, do not go coppicing alone.

is best for this. The left hand is holding the branch and if the saw or bill hook does slip, the gloved hand will be somewhat protected from injury. Fortunately, you are cutting fairly small, round wood with a diameter of no more than 50-100 mm (2-4 in) at the base so the risks can be minimised.

Ensure there are no young children or animals nearby and that you are working in a sufficiently clear area to avoid tripping over stumps and brambles and so on. Once you have identified the stems you want, think about the practicalities. You will probably be cutting upright stems, so consider the direction in which they will fall. Make sure you are well positioned and not leaning your weight against the stem or you could fall. If you are using a pruning saw, the saw blade may get pinched by the weight of the tree as the cut progresses. It is most easily released by pushing the stem away from you, thus taking the downward pressure off the blade.

The twiggy branches at the top tend to get tangled around each other and it is possible to cut several stems with nothing falling as they are held in position by the upper branches. In this case, once the stem is cut, hold it on your shoulder and pull it out of the wood behind you, ensuring it can fall safely on the ground. You might have to shake it to get it free but in this situation, you are more in control of when and where your stem will fall.

Be aware that these trees and saplings are springy, you push in one direction to cut the base of a stem and it can spring back unexpectedly. Keep your tools in an easy-to-find spot as you don't want to trip over any sharp tools unexpectedly and you need to be able to find everything once you have finished. Buy brightly coloured tools so that they are easy to see amongst trees and leaves. Always make sure your tools are clean and sharp as blunt tools are more likely to slip and cause an accident.

Safety in the workshop

There are a few additional safety instructions that apply when you bring back sticks to your workshop.

- Reduce your sticks to manageable lengths before bringing them into the workshop
- Ensure you are working in a clutter-free environment
- Always hold sticks in a vice, workmate, shaving horse or sawing horse before working with them. Round sticks do not easily hold still
- Never attempt to make a tenon on a stick that is not firmly secured
- Never wear open-toed shoes
- Tie back long hair; do not wear scarves, ties or dangling sleeves
- Wear goggles to protect your eyes from bark ribbons when tenoning
- Wear a mask to protect your nose and mouth

Chapter 5

Stools and small tables

5. Stools and small tables

*Whatever is flexible and flowing will tend to grow; whatever
is rigid and blocked will wither and die.*
Lao Tsu

Stools and small tables are quick and satisfying to make. You can make
one in a day, with just a few basic tools, an idea in your head and
inspiration in your heart! Green wood work is not just about the result, it
is about taking your time, carrying out each stage of the process with care
and learning new skills. Be picky, don't say 'oh that will do, who's going
to see it?' If something goes wrong, throw away the stick and find a new
one. It only takes a few extra minutes to replace a component but your
satisfaction will last forever.

Stools are the most versatile pieces of furniture in the house. An adult's
footstool can be a table or seat for a small child or a coffee table if you
happen to be sitting in an armchair. You can use a stool as a seat when
lighting fires or hanging decorations. Take the stool out in the garden and
catch the sunshine. When you have made one stool it will quickly be
appropriated by others and you will have to make another and maybe
another.

I use hazel, birch or alder for stool or table frames (legs, rungs and
stretchers) but none of these woods are suitable for seats as they rarely
grow big enough to be planked. I use hardwood planks for the stool or
table tops. My preference is for waney-edged (natural edged) elm

*below: coffee table, birch with elm top
opposite page: Wiggly legged stool,
hazel and birch with elm top*

because of the wild grain, the colours and hardness of the wood. Avoid soft woods as they have a tendency to split very easily along the grain, usually when you are sitting on them! Suitable native hardwoods are: elm, oak, ash, yew, sycamore, horse chestnut or beech. The plank should be at least 32 mm (1¼ in) thick.

Traditionally, there are two methods for making stools known as slab and stick (such as the traditional three-legged milking stool) and post and rail (a square stool often with rush/rope seat, woven across the top rails).

I have developed a slightly different method for making stools and small tables using unseasoned wood, which incorporates aspects of both traditional methods. Using this approach, you can make anything from a foot stool to a coffee table.

If this is your first, it should be strong, attractive and simple to make. A small, rectangular stool, with approximately 250 mm (10 in) legs, will be useful and when completed, will encourage you to greater challenges. Recommended stool measurements for a first attempt are 250 mm (10 in) wide at one end and 225 mm (9 in) wide at the other end, 375 mm (15 in) long and 400 mm (16 in) high.

below: birch stool with elm top
opposite page: hazel stool
with elm top

Select sticks from hazel that is recently cut and still unseasoned. A diameter of approximately 37.5 mm (1½ in) at the thick end, is ideal for your four legs. If your plank measures more than 32 mm (1¼ in) then select slightly heavier sticks. Play around with this and make the aesthetic decisions yourself.

You can peel the bark or leave it on. If peeled, there will be considerable sanding to do later which some people enjoy and others try to avoid. Some want to peel off all the bark, others will not touch it, they love the colours and the texture. This is personal choice and only you can decide.

> **Making tip:**
> Once you have measured and cut your first leg, use it to measure the next three. Tape measures are tricky to use on round sticks!

> **Design tip:**
> Peeling gives a very different look to a piece. It looks more civilised or 'indoorsy' if the bark is removed. Peeling also opens up the piece. When you look at a stool, or chair that still has its bark on, it is as if you are only seeing the outside of the tree. With white, polished surfaces, the tree seems to open and reveal the wood inside.

If this is your first attempt at making a stool, keep it simple. Use straight-ish legs, maybe with just a little kick or foot at the bottom.

Cut all four legs to the same length.

Select slightly lighter gauge sticks for your rungs and stretcher. The rungs need to be thick enough to drill a 15 mm (⅝ in) hole.

Cutting list
(all measurements are approximate)

Item	Qty	Metric (mm)	Imperial (in)
Posts	4	250	10
Rungs	2	125	5
Stretcher	1	250	10
Seat – plank of ash, elm or oak	1	250 x 375	10 x 15

opposite page: stools in a variety of heights and designs

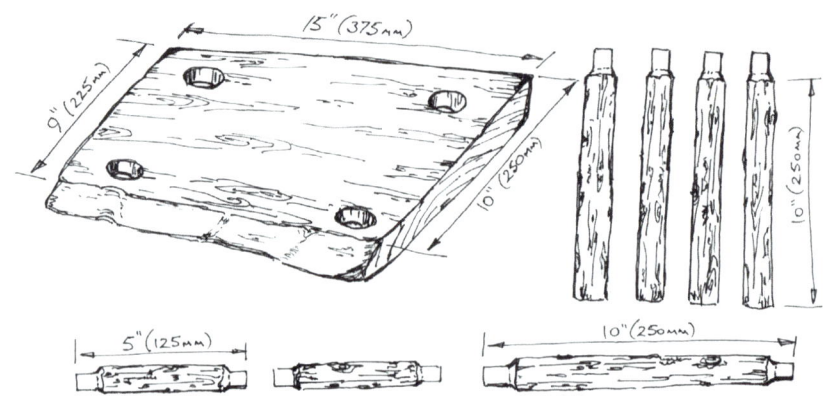

Figure 18

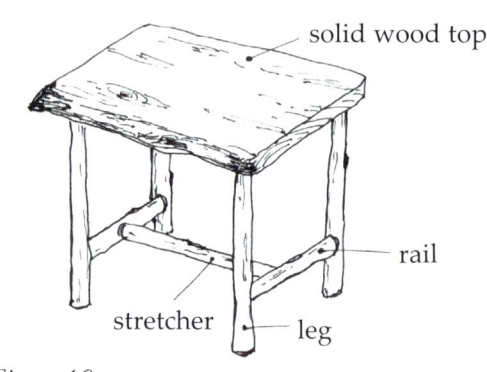

solid wood top

rail

stretcher   leg

Figure 19

Cordless drill and tenoner in action

Method

Stand the legs on the bench (thicker ends towards the ground). Pair them up and decide which way they should face.

On both ends of the two rungs make a 18 mm (¾ in) tenon, approximately 25 mm (1 in) long plus shoulders.

Make 18 mm (¾ in) tenons on top of all four legs. Mark the centre line (highest point) with chalk.

Measure approximately 150 mm (6 in) from the ground on each leg and mark a chalk cross. This is the centre of the stick where you are going to drill.

A pillar drill makes this job easier, you will be surprised at the resistance of green wood to a metal drill bit. Always use a V cradle to hold your sticks as otherwise they may turn or roll.

Once your holes are drilled, assemble the H frames, using PVA glue in the mortices and on the tenons.

Your tenons might require a small amount of whittling (don't get carried away) especially at the top, to persuade them into the mortices. Knock the frames together using a rubber mallet to avoid damaging the bark. If necessary, follow up with a sash clamp which has greater, gentler pressure than a mallet.

top left: marking the
centre line with chalk
top right: measuring and
marking drill holes
left: drilling into the centre point
above: two H frames,
one in sash clamps

Turn your plank (for the top/seat) upside down and mark the positions of the posts for drilling, using the H frames to measure the width.

Drill the holes, using an 18 mm (¾ in) drill bit, to a depth of just over 25 mm (1 in) using the measuring stick to check the depth. Tap the H frames lightly into position and take the measurement for the stretcher that joins

top right: marking drill holes using an H frame
right: measure from centre to centre of rails
page 66:alder and birch chair with elm seat

the two frames together. It should be a few millimetres too long to allow some tension in the stool/table, which makes the structure stronger.

Cut your stretcher to length, make a 15 mm (⅝ in) tenon on each end. Choose which way the H frames should face, drill into the centre of the rungs on each H frame using a 15 mm (⅝ in) drill bit and your measuring stick to check the depth.

Assemble the stool. You already have the two end frames glued and assembled. Apply glue to all the mortices, both of the rungs and the plank for the top. Tap the stretcher into the mortices you drilled into the rungs of the H frames, which gives you an assembled under-frame. With the plank upside down on the bench, and using a wooden mallet, firmly tap each leg into the four holes in the plank. Using just one sash cramp, work around, applying it to each leg and across the length of the stretcher, to make sure that all the tenons are in to the right depth.

Sand the top of the table or stool and apply three coats of Danish oil, lightly sanding between coats.

Making tip:
Once the sash clamp has been used to ensure the tenons have gone all the way in, remove it. You do not need to leave it while the glue dries.

Chapter 6

Side chair

6. Side chair

I had three chairs in my house, one for solitude, two for friendship and three for society.
Henry David Thoreau

Ancient Neolithic remains and artefacts show us that chairs were used by humans as far back as 10,000 years ago. Chairs are ubiquitous yet to most of us chairs are invisible or at least outside of our conscious awareness. In Western civilisations a chair lifts an individual above those around him or her. Unlike benches or reclining divans, a chair keeps an individual separate. High-backed chairs frame the figure of the person sitting in them. They can be turned to face in a particular direction and you can literally turn your back on someone or on a part of the room, unlike stools which are generally more egalitarian pieces of furniture. We

left: hazel dressing chair with upholstered handmade felt seat
opposite page: birch 'torro' chair with elm seat

Green Wood Chairs

Hazel Chair with ash seat

use chairs to sit down to eat, to travel, to work in and also to relax. There is seating at the theatre, the dentist, the library and the cinema.

These chairs mean a lot more in our lives than just a place to sit, we entrust our entire body weight to a chair but we rarely look at them. Chairs can still demonstrate a difference in status such as that between a boss and an employee or an elderly person and a young one. We often stick to one particular chair at the dinner table and in a restaurant; we know that the head of the table is the high status seat.

Traditionally, at a dining table, the two end chairs are armchairs, often called carvers. The rest of the chairs fit neatly around both sides of the

Making tip:
Many of the techniques described in this chapter are basic to chair construction and will not be repeated elsewhere. Refer back to them as you work on the projects in the following chapters of this book.

table and tuck under if necessary. A side chair is simply a basic chair that does not have arms, gaining its name from the way it is placed around the sides of the table. One year, I made nothing but side chairs, wanting to strip my designs back to the basic components, a seat and a back rest. They are very satisfying to make as they are uncluttered and simple. They show off the wood to its best advantage and they only just make the leap from sticks to furniture.

Cutting list

	quantity	metric	imperial (in)
Back posts	2	1.12 m	44
Front posts	2	500 mm	20
Back rails	3	380 mm	15
Front rails	1	457 mm	18
Spindles	4	432 mm	17
Stretchers	4	432 mm	17
Seat height		457 mm	18

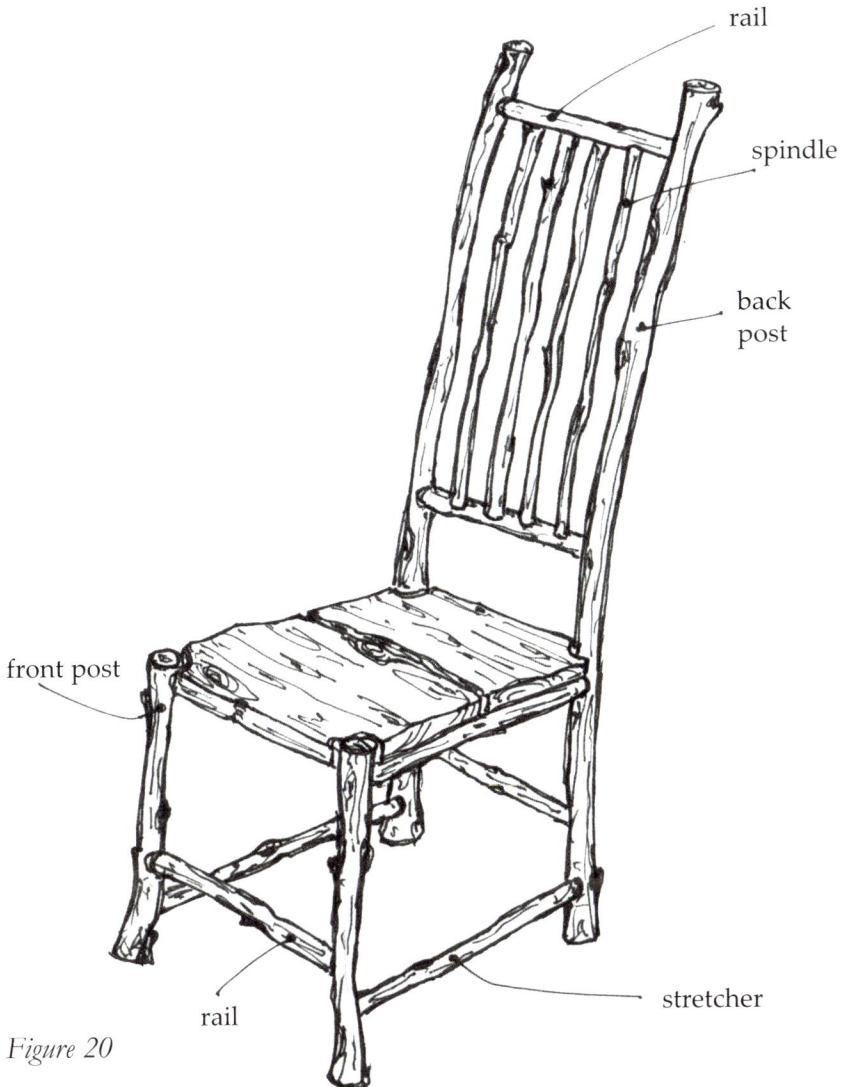

rail

spindle

back post

front post

rail

stretcher

Figure 20

Design tip:
Be careful not to make the back too high as the chair will be unstable, especially if you do not use a wooden seat which gives added weight and stability.

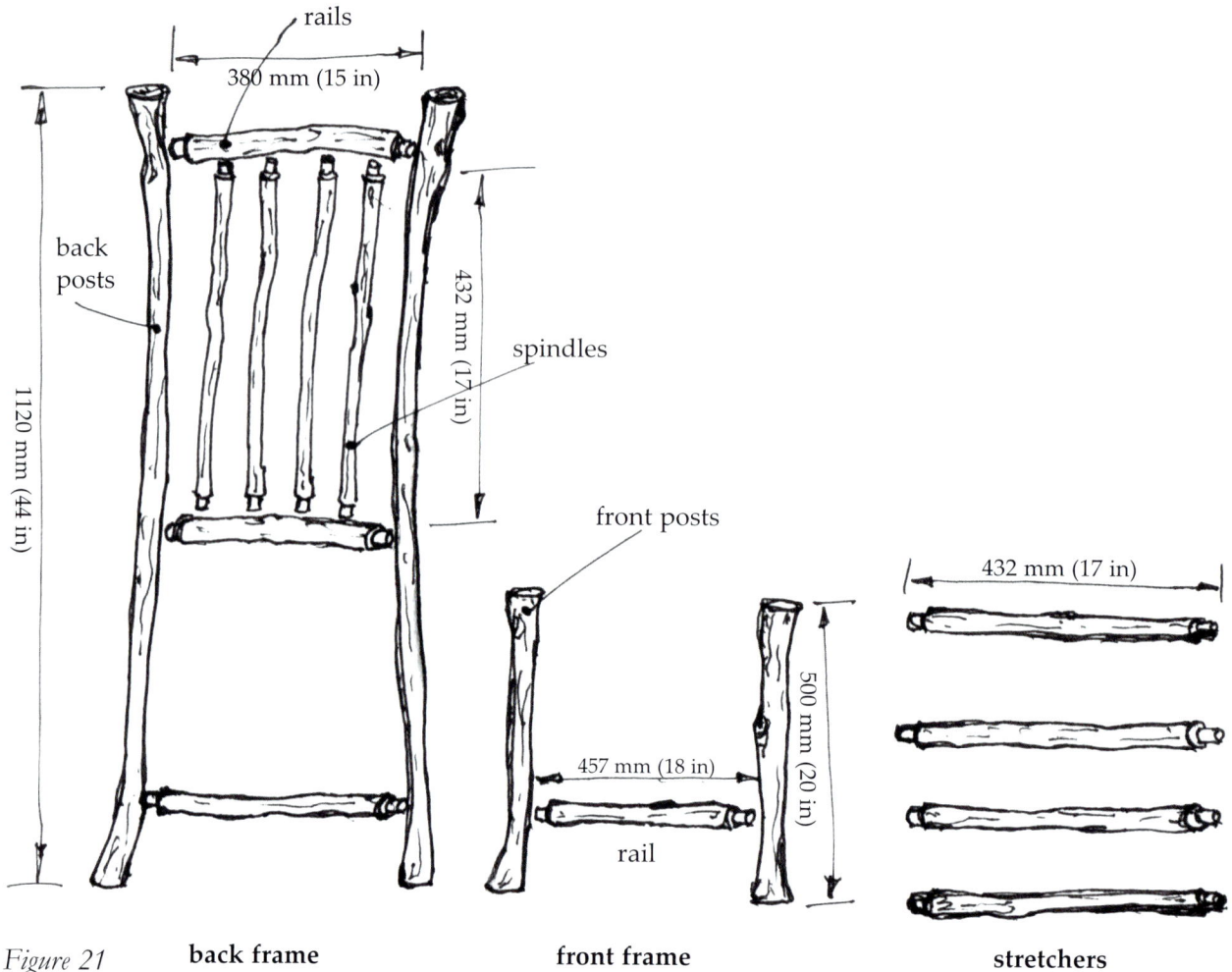

Figure 21   **back frame**   **front frame**   **stretchers**

Although there is a cutting list, **only cut the components for the back frame first.** These are: two back posts, three rails and four spindles. You do not want the wood to dry out too quickly and as soon as it is cut, the drying process speeds up. You may select the material you are planning to use but do not cut it yet.

A chair is made in four stages:
1) Back frame
2) Front frame
3) Join front to back
4) Seat and arms (if making an armchair)

Stage 1 Back frame

Select two back posts of similar thickness, and colour. They should have a slight curve and the curves must match. If you are cutting from long sticks, select your first back post, cut it to length and then compare with the full length sticks for a matching curve.

Put aside your back posts and concentrate on making the back panel.

Using the cordless drill and 18 mm (¾ in) tenoning attachment, put tenons on each end of the three rails. Cut your spindles to length and put 15 mm (⅝ in) tenons on each end of the spindles. Decide which two rails

left: looking for matching curves
right: mark with arrows the face you
will be drilling into

you want to be the top and bottom of the panel. The third rail goes beneath the seat and is not very visible. Strip any of these components if you want stripped bark (see the section on bark stripping in Chapter Four). If you strip the bark off the back or front posts, sand them now and cover them with a layer of Clear Briwax or something similar to seal them and slow down the drying out process. They may be a bit too green to sand effectively so simply wax them and you can remove this before the final sanding.

Find the centre line along the two rails and draw it with a white chalk (see finding the centre point in Chapter Four). Measure for the position of your spindles and mark across the centre line, creating crosses for drilling.

Using the 15 mm (⅝ in) drill bit in your drill press, put the rail in a V cradle and drill four holes, to a depth of approximately 18 mm (¾ in) (use a measuring stick to check depth). Do the same to the other rail. Put the spindles into the holes of one rail (no need for glue), tap them down with a wooden mallet, put the other rail into place and tap down with a rubber mallet so as not to damage the bark.

You should now have a panel made up of two rails and four spindles; you might need to twist it slightly to make it lie flat. Now measure for

Making tip:
Everything is easier when you use straight sticks. Use straight-ish spindles for your first attempt.

> **Design tip:**
> If you intend to weave or upholster a seat, you need an extra rail across both front and back of the chair at seat height. It should be offset by 25 mm (1 in) lower than the side stretchers at front and back.

'square'. Here you want to make certain that it measures the same at each end. With your tape measure check the length from the centre of the top-rail tenon to the centre of the bottom-rail tenon. Do the same on the other side and they should be roughly the same (see figure 22).

If there are significant differences of more than 12.5 mm (½ in), take it apart and check that:

- spindles are all the same length
- the tenons on each end of the spindles are the same length
- the holes are drilled to the same depth

If you still find the same problem after you have checked all these measurements, use a sash clamp to pull the joints firmly together.

The panel now has to be fitted into the back posts. Hold the two back posts together, turning them until you find the best matching curves,

below left: use the panel to mark the top hole for drilling
below right: measure the panel for 'square' from centre of tenons
far below left: use a sash clamp to pull the frame together
far below right: squeeze the panel together by using a sash clamp

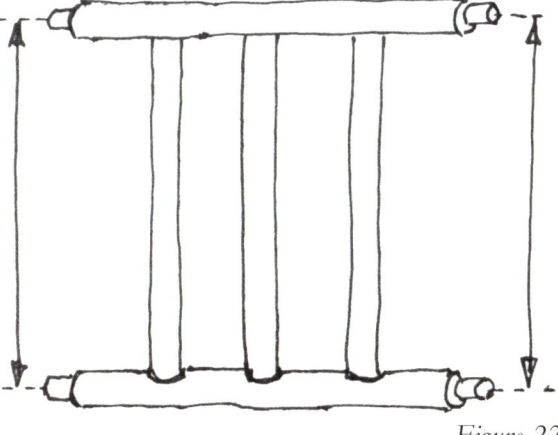

Figure 22

then mark them with arrows on top (this will be your centre line which is the face you drill into). Select your rail material. It should be slightly smaller gauge but still thick enough to drill 15 mm (⅝ in) holes into for your spindles. Cut three rails the same length. Next look for spindles. These can be straight, crooked or forked.

Draw your centre line with a white chalk all the way down the back posts and measure off the height of the holes you are going to drill.

The lowest hole should be 100 mm (4 in) from the bottom end of the stick. The next hole will be at 575 mm (23 in) and the top one at 1 m (40 in). Using a 18 mm (¾ in) bit in your drill press, make a hole on the first and second crosses you have marked with chalk. Do not drill the top hole yet. Do the same with both back posts. Using your panel to measure, put the tenons of the lower rail into their matching holes and mark the place for the top hole. This needs to be measured with the panel itself and not with a tape measure.

Mark and drill the top hole on both back posts, slightly whittle your tenons, then glue and assemble the entire back frame.

Use a sash clamp across each rail to ensure the joints are pulled in as far as they will go, as with the stool, there is no need to leave them on.

Stage 2 Front frame

Select two front posts. To keep things simple use straight-ish posts that are cut at least 50 mm (2 in) over-length to avoid splitting when you assemble the joints. Cut two front posts to length. Cut a front rail. Make a 18 mm (¾ in) tenon on each end of the rail.

Decide which way your posts will face and draw a centre line down the length of the stick (as in Chapter Four). Measure and mark at 100 mm (4 in) from the bottom end of the two posts, forming a cross. When making a chair with a wooden seat, you only need one rail across the front, but it can be an attractive design detail to use two slightly lighter gauge rails.

Using the V cradle and 18mm drill bit, make your mortices to a depth of just over 25 mm (1 in). Lightly whittle your tenons, then glue and assemble the front frame, using a sash clamp across the joints to ensure they are in as deep as possible.

Design tip:
The front rail is a good place to use interesting details. You often find sticks with strange anomalies which don't affect the strength of the component. If used sparingly they add interest to the piece.

Stage 3 Joining the front frame to the back frame

Make four stretchers to join the back and front frames together. Select the straightest sticks you can find. This is important because crooked stretchers will prevent your chair's feet from touching the ground, creating a chair that rocks but not in a good way! Cut all four stretchers to a length of 425 mm (17 in) and make a 18 mm (¾ in) tenon on both ends. Look at your finished back frame and note which way it slopes back. A comfortable chair requires a back rest that curves slightly away from your back when sitting down.

Place your back frame on the bench and mark the centre line with white chalk on both back posts. Using a tape measure, mark the positions of the mortices, 125 mm (5 in) and 425 mm (17 in) from the bottom of the posts.

Place your front frame on the bench and mark it in the same way for drilling with holes at the same heights.

Making tip:
If you are going to use two rails across the front, they should be a minimum of 60 mm (2½ in) apart.

77

Mark drilling holes on front frame

As the front of the chair is wider than the back, the stretchers need to flare out from the back, therefore the mortice holes need to be drilled at an angle. This process cannot be easily done using a pillar drill. Place your back frame on the floor or a low bench. Using a cordless drill and 18 mm (¾ in) drill bit, start drilling holding your drill straight, at a 90 degree angle to the wood.

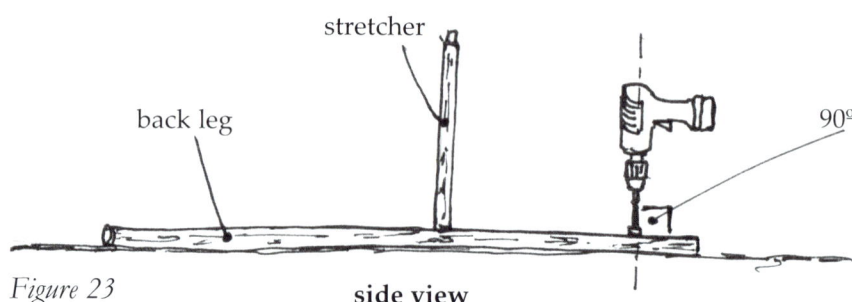

stretcher

back leg

90º

Figure 23   **side view**

Once the bit starts to cut, gently pull the drill out to a slight angle. It only needs to be the smallest of angles and you cannot measure it accurately.

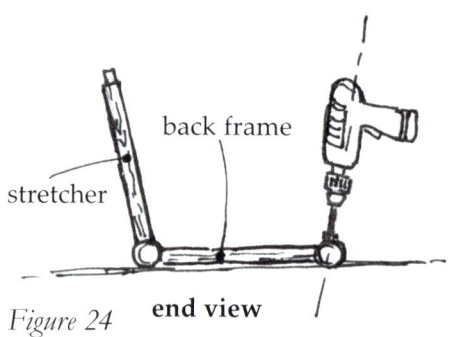

back frame

stretcher

Figure 24   **end view**

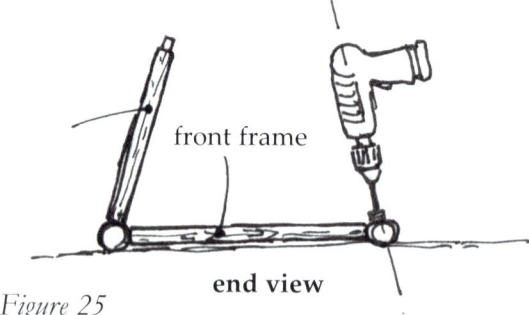

front frame

Figure 25   **end view**

Making tip:

Make sure you do not drill the wrong side because it is quite uncomfortable if the back of the chair slopes towards you.

If you are worried about keeping the same angle, after drilling one hole, put a stretcher into the mortice, you then have a stick to line up your drill with for the second hole. You will find it is quite difficult to drill into green wood but if you lay the frame on the floor the added body weight behind the drill makes for more successful drilling. Use your measuring stick (see Chapter Four) for checking the depth of the mortices. Repeat this procedure for the front frame, this time bringing the angle in. Once the drill starts to cut, keep the angle to a minimum and always keep the drill at 90 degrees to the post.

Lightly whittle your tenons and tap them into position using a wooden mallet. Tap first into the back frame then place the front frame on top of the stretchers. Locate the tenons in the mortices and tap them in using a rubber mallet. This is a dry assembly so do not push the tenons in as far as they can go, you are checking that nothing serious is wrong at this point. Stand the chair up. If the feet are not all touching the ground, give the whole structure a bit of a twist until it is sitting flat-ish.

Mark your stretchers with white chalk on top, so that after you take the chair apart again, you can reconstruct it in the same way. Glue your mortices and tenons, and after tapping all the components together, use a sash clamp to ensure that each tenon has gone in as deep as possible. When you have a three-dimensional chair, and before attaching the seat, you will need to sand all the parts that have been stripped. I use a medium grade (120 grit), emery cloth, torn into strips to sand the round components. Wrap the strip around the spindle, hold one end in each hand and pull each end alternately. This way the components keep their

Alder side chair with leather upholstered seat

roundness while you sand them. On larger, flatter parts of the chair such as the arms, I use an electric palm sander which is dusty and noisy but speeds the job up considerably. The final sanding should be done by hand with a fine (240) emery cloth. A Clear Briwax finish has a wonderful mellow sheen but is a bit impractical because any water that touches the seat turns the polish white. It is easy to lightly sand it back and re-polish but, depending on how your chair is used, it can be high maintenance. Danish oil gives a more practical, functional finish. It protects the wood and can be wiped clean with a damp cloth.

If the wood you have been working with is very green, give the stripped bark a covering of Clear Briwax or similar, to prevent it from drying out too quickly. The larger the component, the more important this is. Before I attach the arms I sometimes give them a covering of Briwax as soon as they are stripped (with special attention to the cut ends). This slows down the seasoning process and prevents cracking. The wax then has to be removed, using a coarse sand paper, before the final finishing and sanding.

Stage 4 Seat and arms

If your chair is to have a wooden seat, you need one or two planks measuring at least 450 mm (18 in) deep, 475 mm (19 in) wide and no more than 25 mm (1 in) thick. The plank must fit around the front posts and not sit behind them. You do not want straight lines. If you have a plank with straight edges, you will want to 'spoil' or shape the edge either by sanding, cutting or rasping. Use two small planks as it is easier to fit the seat in two parts. Cut the plank roughly to size, then placing the front edge in position, draw the shape of the front posts onto the seat material. Cut them out using a jig saw or a fret saw and tidy up the shapes using a rounded micro plane.

Make final adjustments to the shape and fit of the seat, allowing the seat to cover the side rails (stretchers) but without too much of an overhang. Sand all the underneath surfaces and edges before attaching the seat. Using a plug cutter, cut four for a single plank, (or eight for two planks) using the waste material from the seating plank.

Once you have the seat made, attach it in three steps:

- Mark with crosses where your screws will go (not too close to the edge, you want them to go through the seat and into the stretchers at the highest point). Drill a counter-sink hole, about 12.5 mm (½ in) deep using a size 10 drill bit.
- Using a fine twist-drill bit, drill all the way through but not into the stretcher.
- Put the seat into position and using 4 x 30 mm (1¼ in) screws, screw it down, tightening each screw just enough to hold, then go back round again tightening each screw fully.

Dip the plugs into a little glue and tap them into the countersunk holes using a light hammer. If they are standing proud, turn the chair on its back and using a very fine tooth saw, cut them short, then sand flat.

Making tip:
This is a precaution to prevent any chance of cracking due to drying out too quickly. However, even without wax, the stripped components do not usually crack.

opposite page: birch side chair with cherry seat
below: shape seat around posts using a microplane

right: make plugs of same wood to cover screw heads
opposite page: three side chairs, hazel with elm seats
page 84: Jeremy Irons with his own green wood chair

If you wish to scoop out and shape the seat for comfort, use a travisher or adze or even a large carving gouge. You can shape the seat simply by rasping, using micro planes or a spoke shave or sanding the edges, especially along the front edge where the legs overhang the seat. If using power tools, a sanding disc on an angle grinder is very effective but also creates a lot of dust so a mask is essential.

Seating can be made using a wide variety of materials. One student used a fur coat bought in a second-hand shop and created a beautiful child's chair with a furry seat and back rest! Use your ingenuity to discover new methods for seating chairs. I regularly work with leather and wood but chairs can be upholstered, rush-seated, caned or woven with súgán. The choices are limited only by the materials you can find and your skills in using them. I recommend *Chair Seating Techniques in Cane, Rush, Willow and Cords* by Mary Butcher, Kay Johnson and Olivia Elton Barratt for those who wish to weave seats onto their chairs.

Safety tip:
Fine wood dust is carcinogenic. Always wear a mask when sanding and change your clothes after finishing work. Cut down on the amount of time you are continuously inhaling the dust.

Making tip:
When a spindle has touched the base of a mortice hole it gives a different sound when hit with a mallet. There will be a dead sound as opposed to a slight resonance when air is still trapped in the hole.

Chapter 7

Child's chair

7. Child's chair

'There was a heap of sticks on the other side of the wood', said Piglet, 'I saw them, lots and lots, all piled up.'
House at Pooh Corner
A.A. Milne

Children love to have small sized chairs that have been made specially for them. Why do we expect children to be satisfied with plastic when children respond strongly to tactile experiences and love touching and exploring natural materials? As a child I loved tree houses and dens made of branch wood. My first pocket money was spent on a penknife which I used to peel sticks with!

These chairs work very well on a small scale, because there is something faerie-like about them. I know adults who still own the chair they had as a child, so any faerie chairs you make may become family heirlooms. One of the pleasures of making these tiny chairs is that each one can be personalised, you can make simple or more complex designs, depending on your skill, experience and the sticks you brought back from the woods. The following project is a suitable size for toddlers and as it is not an armchair, they will never grow too big to sit on it.

Cutting list

Item	Qty	Metric (mm)	Imperial (in)
Back posts	2	530	21
Front posts	2	250	10
Back rails	3	180	7
Front rail	1	280	11
Spindles	3	200	8
Stretchers	4	250	10
Seat height		240	9½

opposite page: child's hazel side chair, elm seat

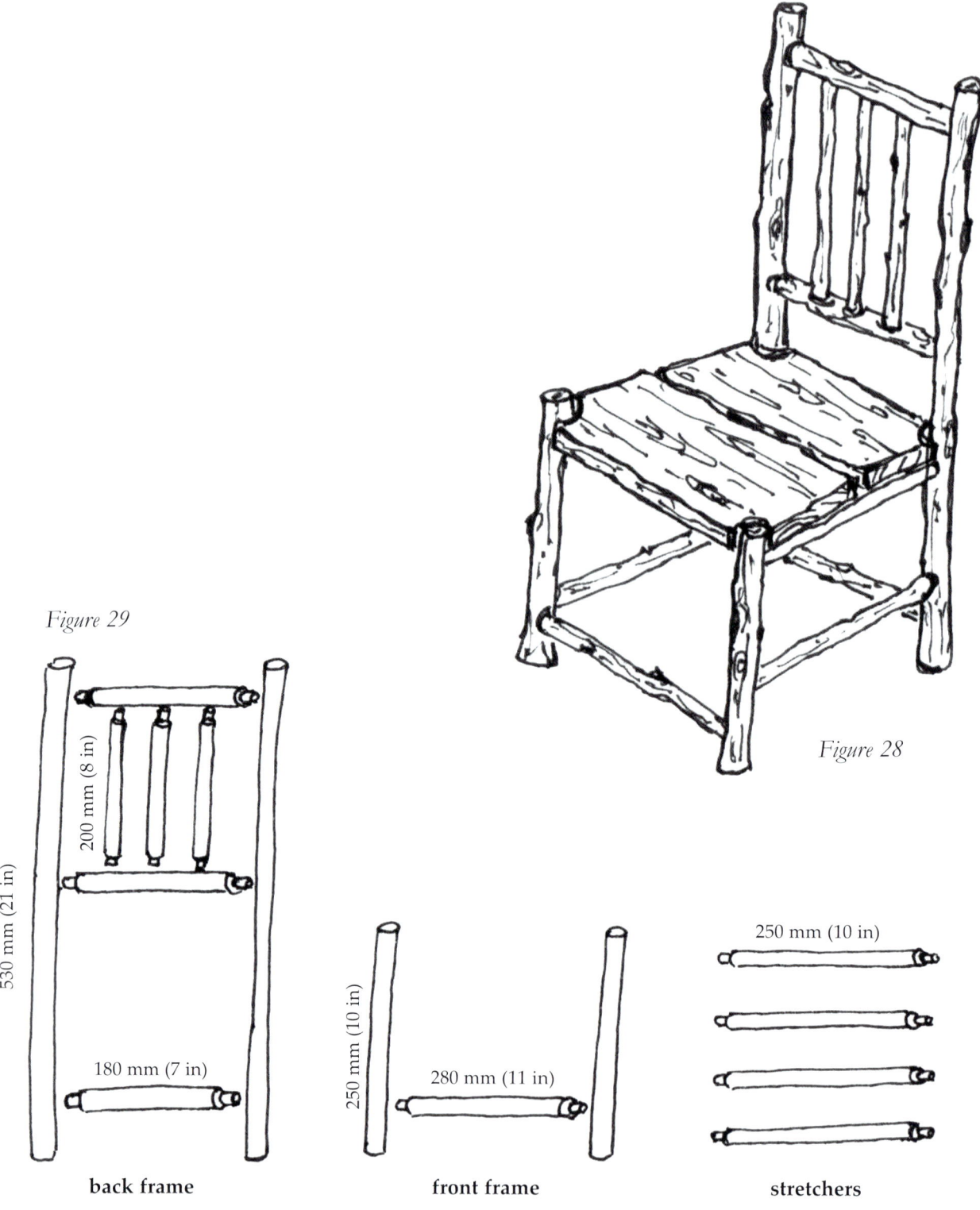

Figure 29

Figure 28

200 mm (8 in)

530 mm (21 in)

180 mm (7 in)

back frame

250 mm (10 in)

280 mm (11 in)

front frame

250 mm (10 in)

stretchers

The making process is identical to the stages already described in the previous chapter but the dimensions are different. Work through stages 1, 2 and 3, as detailed in Chapter 6 – The Side Chair.

Stage 4 Wooden Seat

If your chair is to have a wooden seat, you need to find an off cut or small plank measuring at least 250 mm (10 in) deep, 300 mm (12 in) wide and less than 25 mm (1 in) thick. As with the adult side chair, the plank should be shaped to fit around the posts and not sit behind them. The technique for fitting the seat is the same as in the previous chapter.

Making and fitting the arms

Adding arms can be easily done. Simply follow the stages for making the front frame of a side chair but instead of making two front posts measuring 250 mm (10 in) make two front posts measuring 375 mm (15 in) and put a 18 mm (¾ in) tenon on top of each one. Assemble the front panel in the same way.

Make the arms from similar gauge material to the back posts. I use sticks with a slight curve so that the arms are embracing (they are normally slightly thinner towards the back of the chair). You may want to strip the bark and sand the arms, leaving a smooth, strokable surface.

Remember that the arms do not have to match. Our brains are used to seeing manufactured, perfectly symmetrical furniture. Be playful with the arms, use a piece of curvy wood on one side and something different on the other. Let go of preconceived ideas of what a chair should look like, give yourself permission to try something different! I always strip the bark from the arms because people love to explore the sanded, polished surface with their hands.

Hazel and ash
Windsor style baby chair

Arms

On an adult chair, the gap between seat height and the arms is normally 200 mm (8 in). This allows you to rest your elbows comfortably on the surface of the arms without raising or lowering your shoulders. When measuring for the arms, leave an extra overhang that you will cut back later. I do this for two reasons:

- The arms may be very green and the last inch or so might crack
- When you are tapping the arm down onto the tenon of the front post the arm may crack if it is a tight fit unless you have an overhang of 80 mm (3 in) or more.

Cut 2 x 300 mm (12 in) long. Put a 18 mm (¾ in) tenon on the back end of each arm.

Once the seat is attached and sanded lay the chair down on its back. Measure from the seat to the top of the front posts, transfer that measurement onto the back post and mark with a cross. Using an 18 mm (¾ in) drill bit, drill a hole to a depth just over 18 mm (¾ in). Whittle the tenons slightly, lay the chair on its back and using a wooden mallet, tap

opposite page: Hazel child's armchair elm seat
below: Ana with tiny ash armchair

them smartly into place. When the arms are in as deep as they will go, position them above the front post tenons and draw around the tenons, using a sharp, soft pencil. This gives you the exact position for drilling.

Wiggle the arms out of their holes and, using the pillar drill and V cradle, drill the hole you have marked to a depth of just over 18 mm (¾ in). Glue the tenons and the mortices and repeat the process, laying the chair on its back to put the arms into the back posts and standing it up to tap them down onto the tenons. Clean off excess glue. The stripped surfaces of the chair should be thoroughly sanded and treated with Danish oil.

*opposite page: hazel child's
armchair, elm seat
left: hazel child's side chair, elm seat
following page: hazel armchair
with small birch table, elm seat
and table top*

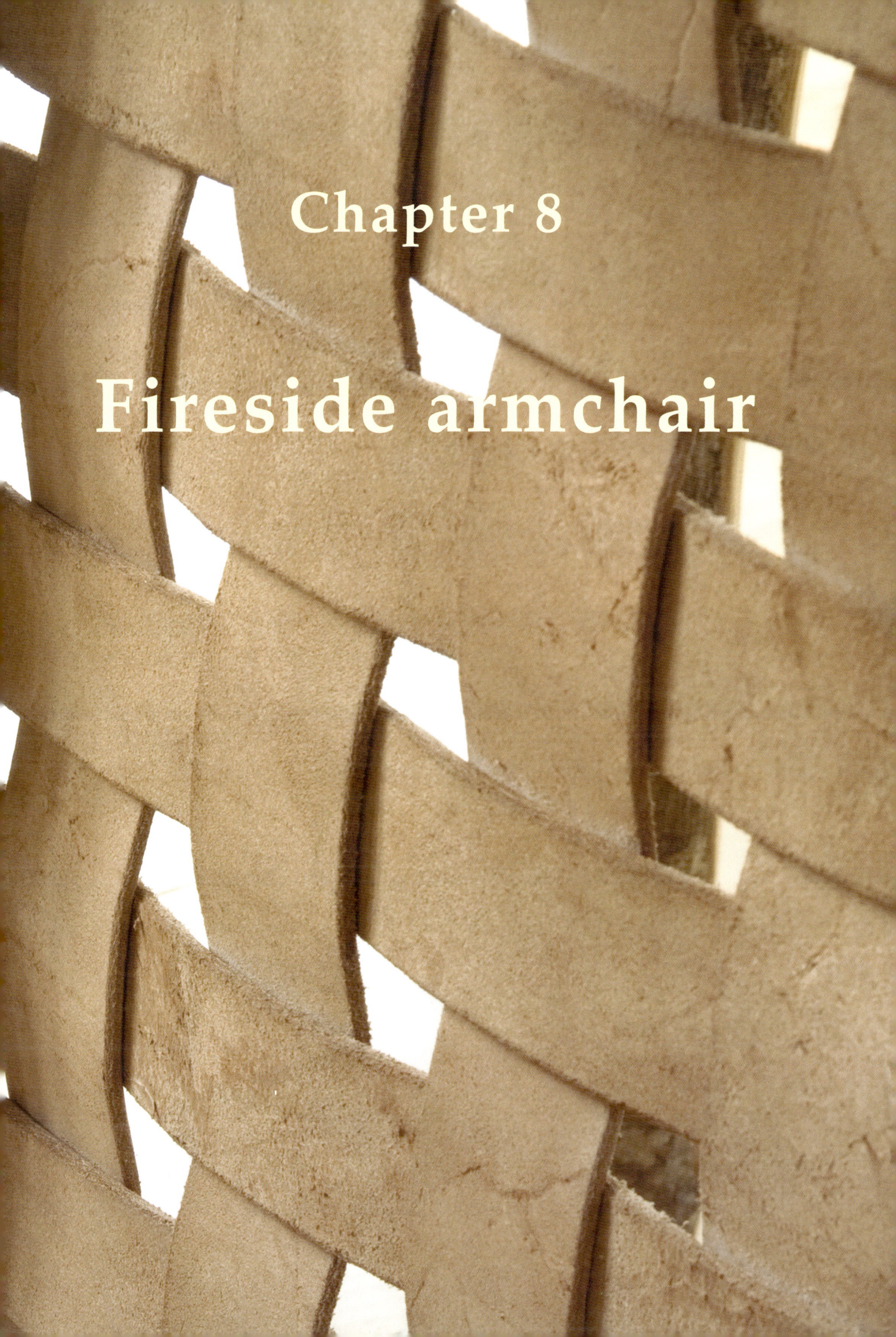

Chapter 8

Fireside armchair

8. Fireside armchair

I dream of...an art of balance...of something like a good armchair
in which one rests from physical fatigue...
Matisse

Relaxing in a comfortable chair beside the fire is one of life's simple pleasures. When we dream of being warm and cosy, a fireside armchair inevitably forms part of the scenario These chairs are designed with relaxation in mind and the seat needs to be soft and comfortable. It can be made with a wooden seat but you will probably end up putting a cushion on it. The ideal solution for extra comfort is a leather seat. This is a Spanish colonial design influence that comes from my time in Colombia where most chairs have leather seats, some with single pieces while others have straps. Leather is a natural material that is unsurpassed. It is ideal seating material because despite its strength and hard wearing properties, it is also soft and comfortable. Natural wood and leather are well suited and look great together, both wear in and develop a patina with use. I am not a skilled leather worker but I have developed a way of making seats using a basic strap design which looks good and works very well on a fireside chair.

Item	Qty	Metric (mm)	Imperial (in)
Back posts	2	990-1000	36-40
Back rails	4	560	22
Spindles	4	500	20
Front posts	2	560	22
Front rails	2	560	22
Stretchers	4	560	22
Arms	2	660	26

opposite page: hazel fireside armchair leather strap seat (felt cushion by Helen Stringer)

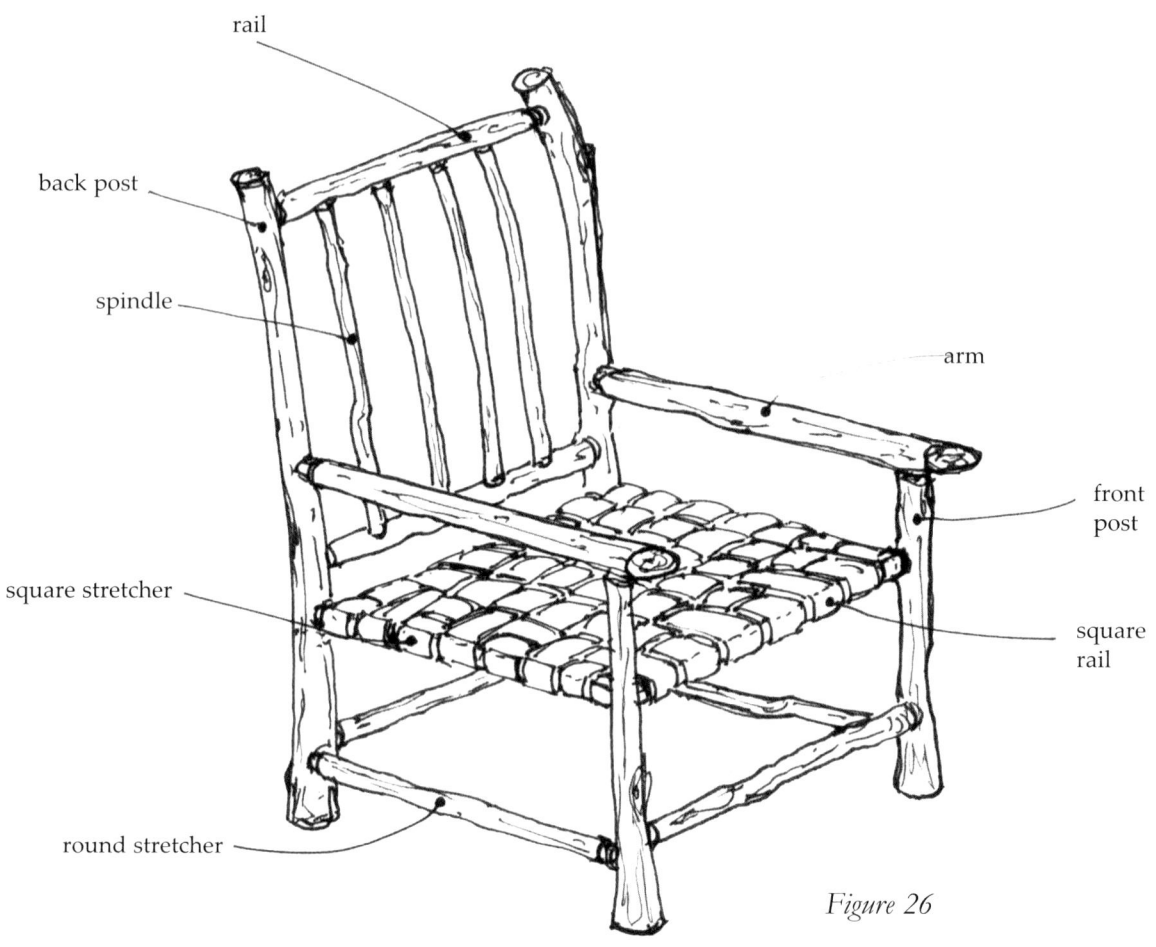

rail

back post

spindle

arm

square stretcher

front post

square rail

round stretcher

Figure 26

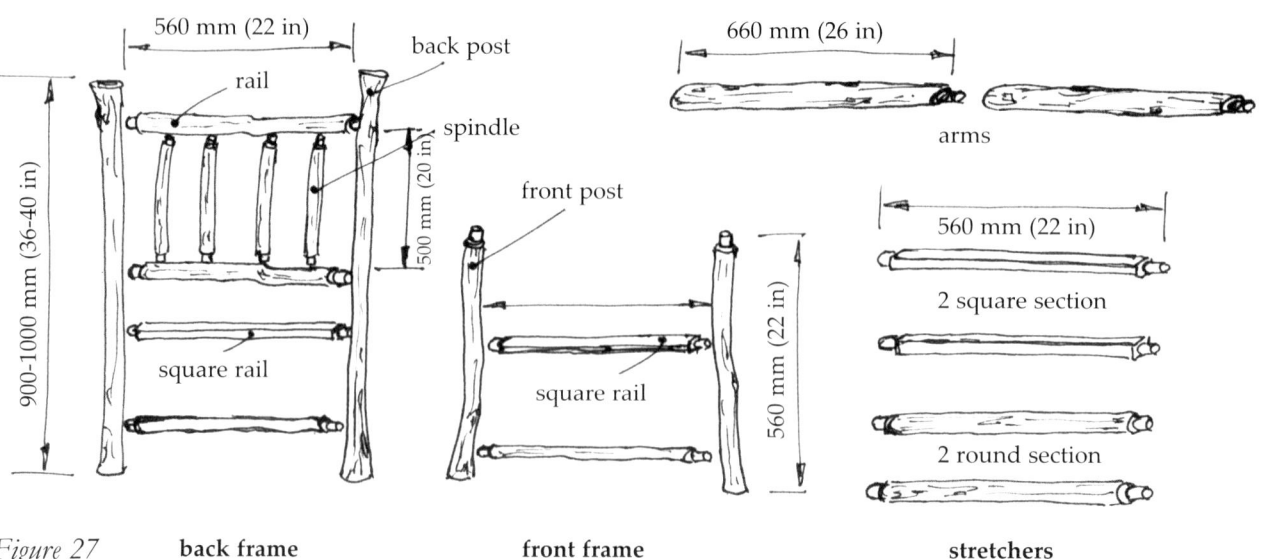

560 mm (22 in)

back post

rail

spindle

500 mm (20 in)

900-1000 mm (36-40 in)

square rail

front post

square rail

560 mm (22 in)

660 mm (26 in)

arms

560 mm (22 in)

2 square section

2 round section

Figure 27   **back frame**   **front frame**   **stretchers**

Cutting list

This chair can be made with slightly heavier wood. I use sticks that have a diameter of around 50 mm (2 in) at the base. Once you have selected enough suitable sticks for making your chair, follow the three stages of construction for the basic side chair in Chapter Six but with two fundamental differences:

Firstly, you need an extra rail across at seat height for both front and back frames. This is because you need a rail all the way around in order to

Low fireside chair, leather straps seat

weave the leather straps. You cannot put the rail at the same height on the front and back as on the two sides because they need to be offset by an inch, lower than the side rails. I use square section wood for the seat rails as it is easier to screw the leather straps into.

Secondly, as this is an armchair, the front posts need to measure 200 mm (8 in) above seat height to support the arms. When the chair is finished and the leather seat is attached, you can attach the arms (see Chapter Seven).

Attach the leather straps to form a woven seat when the structure of your chair is finished but before adding the arms. I use shoulder leather that is 4 mm (³⁄₁₆ in) thick. Cut it into straps using a strap cutter or a metre-long straight edge and a sharp knife.

The straps should be 37.5 mm (1½ in) wide and 675 mm (27 in) long. Cut 20 straps. Using a sharp knife, take off the corners of the strap at each

opposite page: fireside 'Colombia' chair, stretched leather seat below: hazel fireside chair leather strap seat and piglet

opposite page: large hazel
'Farmers' armchair
below: hazel armchair elm seat,
baby chair with rush seat

opposite page: hazel armchair, rush seat
above : detail showing leather straps attached with screw and brass cups
following page: high backed hazel armchair, elm seat

end, leaving them slightly D-shaped, like the tapered end of a belt. Use screws and brass cups to secure the straps to the side rail, work across the seat leaving a gap of approximately 12.5 mm (½ in) between each one.

Attach all ten straps to one side of the chair then wet the straps with a sponge. Stretch each strap one at a time and secure on the other side using the same screw and brass cup fixtures. As the straps dry out they shrink slightly, giving a tight, flat seat that does not sag when you sit down. Repeat the process, working from front to back and weaving the straps up and over the crossways straps. When all the straps are secure, trim off excess ends with a sharp knife.

The leather straps can be finished with Neatsfoot oil which prevents marking.

This design also makes a lovely dog bed if you make the legs shorter so that it is closer to the ground, lower the arms and back rest and add a cushion.

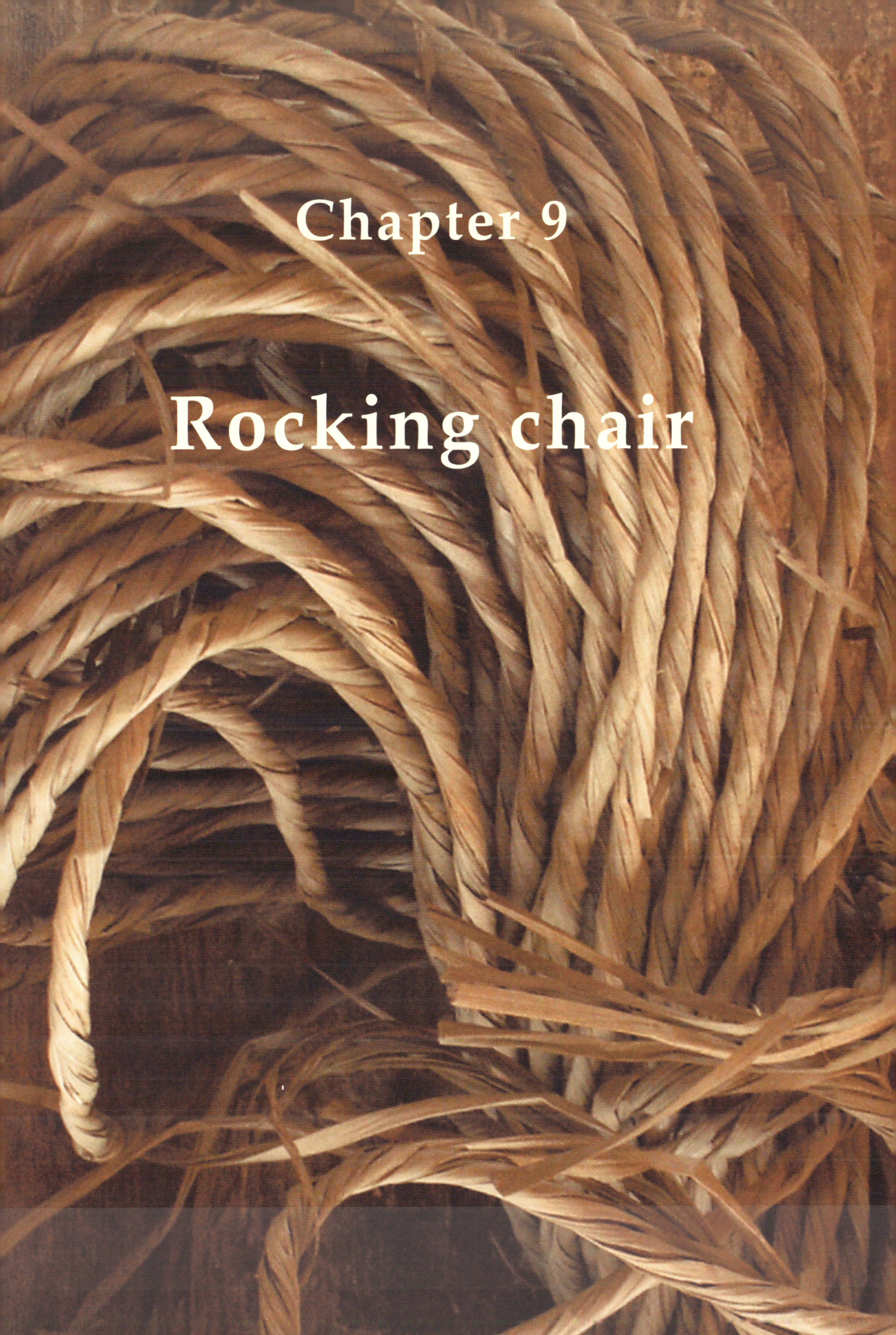

Chapter 9

Rocking chair

9. Rocking chair

"wither I goest - it goes"
JFK famously said about his rocking chair

Rocking chairs appeared in Scandinavia, Europe and the United States in the mid-1700s. They have continued to be popular ever since and have become iconically connected to famous people, most notably Benjamin Franklin and John F. Kennedy and, of course, Whistler's Mother is arguably one of the most famous paintings of a rocking chair. After a tiring day, it is so relaxing to close your eyes and drift away in your own, hand-made rocking chair. Ergonomically, the rocker is supportive to the back, which is why JFK (who suffered with serious back pain) had one in almost every room. At a deeper level, the rocking motion takes us back to early life when we were soothed in a cradle or in our mother's arms.

A green wood rocker can be contemporary and appeal to all tastes and ages. It is the one item of furniture that is generally accepted as not

left: hazel rocker, elm seat
opposite page: birch rocker cherry seat

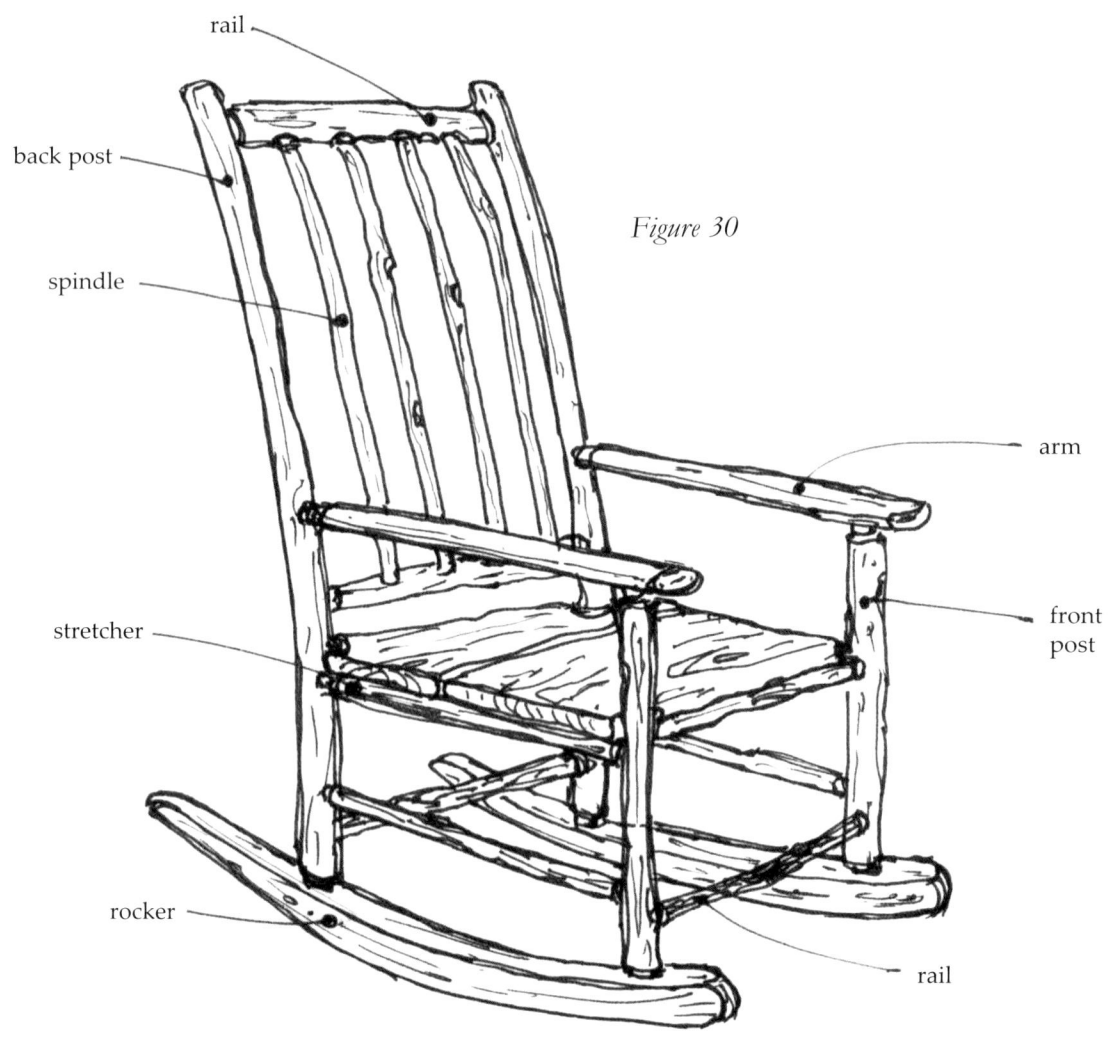

rail

back post

spindle

stretcher

rocker

Figure 30

arm

front post

rail

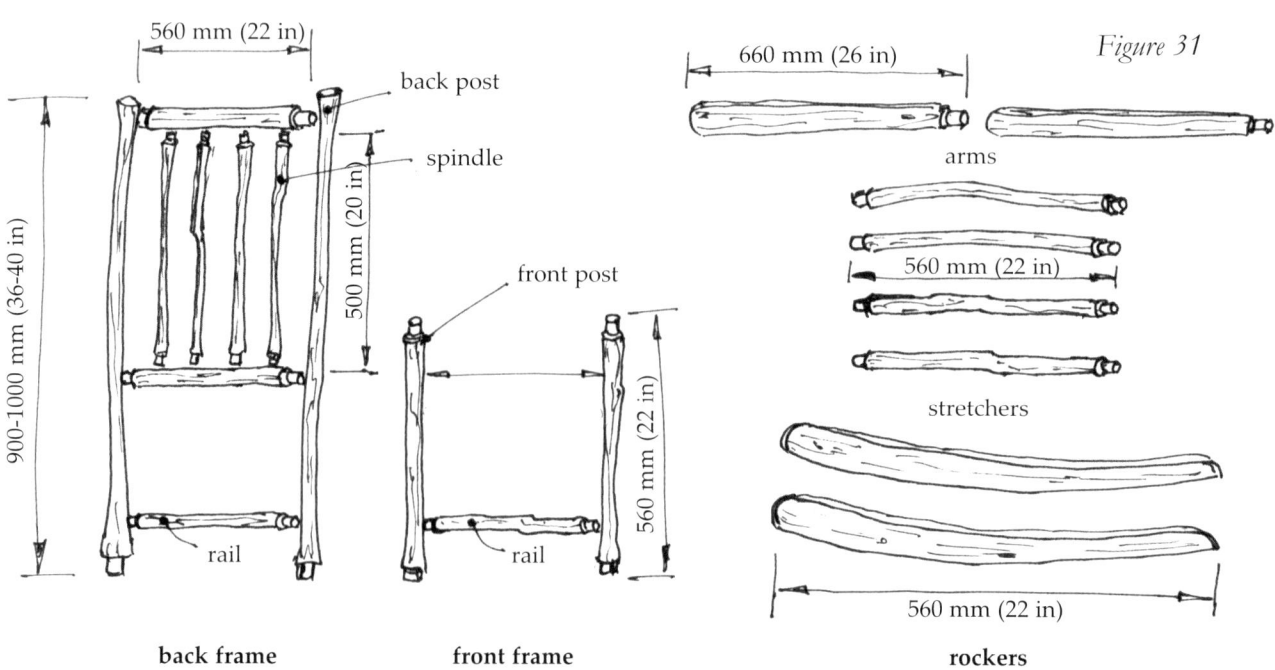

560 mm (22 in)

back post

spindle

500 mm (20 in)

900-1000 mm (36-40 in)

rail

back frame

front post

rail

560 mm (22 in)

front frame

660 mm (26 in)

Figure 31

arms

560 mm (22 in)

stretchers

560 mm (22 in)

rockers

having to match with the rest of the décor. A rocking chair can be a one-off, stand-alone piece, even better if it has personality and is a little quirky. It will say more about its owner than a three-piece suite.

Making a rocking chair using green wood is more of a challenge than making other chairs. In order for the rocking motion to be smooth and comfortable there are certain things that must be correct and even symmetrical, which are not important considerations with non-rockers.

The chair needs to be relatively square without kicking feet or legs, so that the actual rockers run parallel to each other and are not at odd angles. The two rockers must be identical in order for the chair to rock smoothly. Any slight anomaly or difference in shape will result in skewed rocking which is certainly not soothing! However, there are green wood chair makers out there who use curved branches as rockers.

Cutting list

Hazel chair, rush rope seat

Item	Qty	Metric (mm)	Imperial (in)
Back posts	2	1000	40
Back rails	3	375	15
Spindles	4	500	20
Front posts	2	530	21
Front rail	1	560	22
Stretchers	4	475	19
seat height		330	13
seat – solid wood	1	600 wide x 560 deep	24 wide x 22 deep
Arms	2	530	21
Rockers	2	see note immediately below	

If possible the same material should be used for the rockers as the seat. The rockers should measure at least 25 mm (1 in) – not the nominal 25 mm (1 in) after planing.

The seat of a rocking chair is always a few inches lower to allow for the additional height when the chair is set onto its rockers. The ideal dimensions for a chair that will not take up too much floor space are listed on page 111.

Make your chair following the instructions for basic technique in Chapter Six. Keep in mind that the front posts are longer so that the arms can be attached (unless you want to make a rocking side chair). Instructions for making and fitting arms are in Chapter Seven. Do note that the seat height is lower. Make and fit the seat as described in Chapter Six.

opposite page: hazel rocker, elm seat
left: alder rocker, stretched leather seat

right: hazel rocker, elm seat
opposite page: hazel rocker,
nubuck upholstered seat

Making tip:

When making tenons on the end of the back and front posts, lay your chair down on its back, against a wall, and use the tenoner in the usual way.

Do not steady the post with your spare hand. If the tenoner slips and catches the arm that is in front of it, you could get injured.

Rockers

If you do not have access to an existing rocking chair the shape on page 117 can be scaled to your requirement. Turn the chair on its side and literally draw around the rockers, directly onto your plank. When your chair is completed, make a 18 mm (¾ in) tenon on the bottom of each of the four posts. Make sure these tenons point straight down, however curved your back posts are. The tenons will have to fit into holes drilled into the rockers.

Once you have the shape of your rockers drawn directly onto the wood, cut them out using a band saw. Your blade should be at least 12.5 mm (½

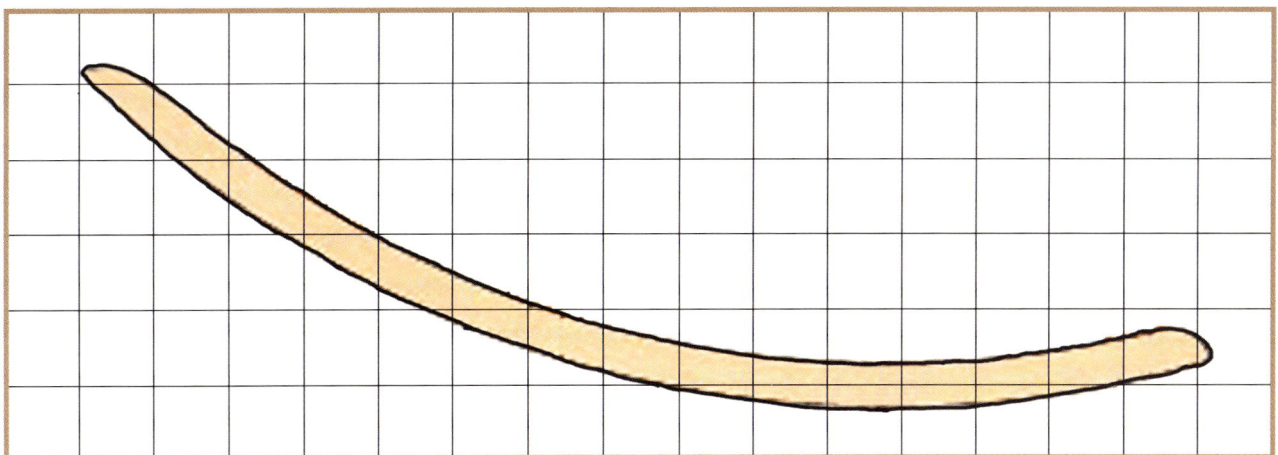

in) wide in order to cut a strong, sweeping curve. Sand all surfaces thoroughly, put the two rockers together and sand as if they were one component so that they are identical. Stand your chair on the rockers, with the tenons of both front posts 63 mm (2½ in) from the front of the rocker. Ensure that the tenons are positioned into the centre of the rocker and draw carefully around them.

Drill the two mortices you have marked into the rockers using a pillar drill. Position the rocker onto the drilling table and place a small wedge under the back and front so that it does not rock while drilling. Ensure that you drill exactly into the centre of the rocker. Drill the holes at least 18 mm (¾ in) deep.

Place the chair onto the rockers with the front tenons in holes. Draw around the rear tenons and repeat the drilling process for the back holes. Attach the rockers with glue and tap into position with a wooden mallet. Ensure that they are on as far as they will go. It may be necessary to pull rockers into position using a sash cramp from the seat to the rocker.
.
Thoroughly sand the seat and rockers as well as any stripped surfaces. Apply two to three coats of Danish oil or Clear Briwax, as necessary.

above: rocker template
opposite page: hazel rocker,
upholstered handmade felt seat
(felt by Helen Stringer)
left: detail hazel back frame and post
following page: hazel rocker, leather
upholstered seat

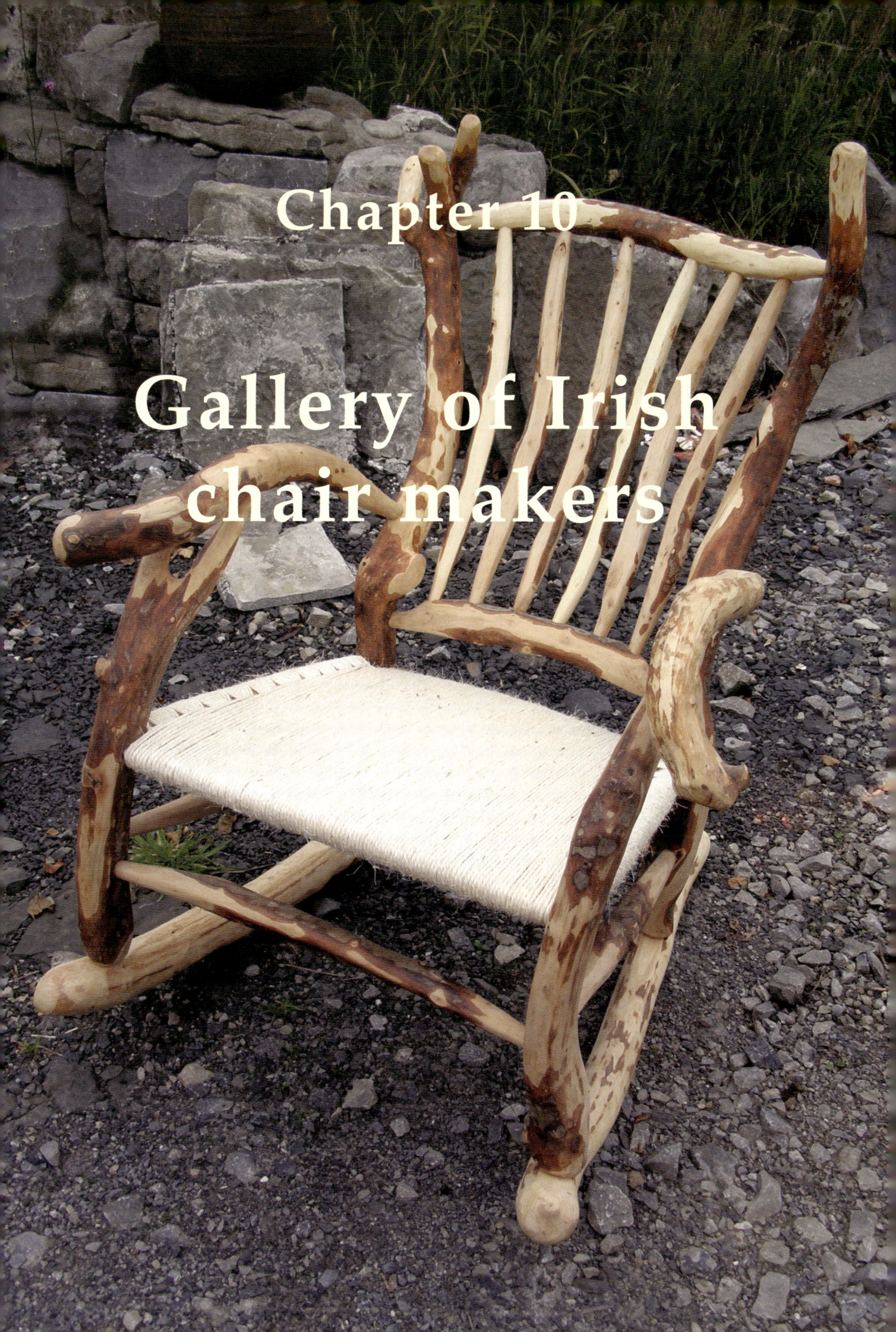

Chapter 10

Gallery of Irish chair makers

10. Gallery of Irish chair makers

Most chair makers in Ireland are quite distinct from furniture makers. They generally work on their own, in small home-based workshops, set up primarily with tools, equipment and space suitable for chair making. They are capable of make stools, tables and other furniture, but clearly, the passion lies in making chairs. Some larger scale furniture producers also make chairs but they find them quite labour-intensive, and difficult to make financially viable.

John and Gabriel Blake

Corrib Crafts
Tuam
County Galway

Tel. 00 353 (0)93 24113

The exception that proves the rule is Corrib Crafts, a medium sized workshop and show-room based in an old church building in Tuam. It has been run for the last 22 years by John and Gabriel.

Corrib Crafts is reminiscent of the enterprises run by Shaker communities in the late 19th century where particular designs were produced partly by machine and by hand, and sold in large quantities. This design is known both as a Sligo or Tuam Chair. Its main characteristics being the single wide board down the back and the T-shaped stretcher joining the back board to the two front legs. The seat is made up from several small components. It may have developed in response to the small amounts of timber available for furniture making 200-300 years ago. Three-legged chairs were popular as many homes had uneven floors and three legs will always touch the ground.

above:
John and Gabriel Blake at work
left: Tuam arm chair in oak
far left: Tuam side chair in oak

Ray Walsh

Old Road, Ballycar
Newmarket on Fergus
County Clare

Tel. 00 353 (0)61 368283
rayxwalsh@yahoo.com
www.chairsandthings.com

Ray Walsh is a retired teacher who makes Windsor-style chairs. His workshop is next to his home and he has piles of wood air-drying in several places around the house as well as in the three kilns he has in the garden.

Ray sources his wood locally, looking out for trees that have been recently felled, to ensure that he can make certain the planking is done correctly. Before starting to work with a particular piece of timber, he checks out the grain 'in three dimensions' looking for curved grain to use for the curved arms of his chairs.

Ray firmly believes in the principle of using a variety of timbers for the jobs that they do best, elm or beech for the seats, ash for the spindles or legs. He also seeks out the beauty of the grain, so that in looking at the chair, the eye sees the most attractive surface of the wood.

Ray's chairs are classic windsor designs, carried out with precision and harmony. In order to facilitate working alone in a home workshop, he has created many ingenious jigs and tools that allow him to be involved in the whole process from cut tree to finished chair.

His goal is to make the perfect chair and he devotes hours to sourcing the wood, building the kilns and inventing the jigs that make that goal a possibility.

Windsor Chairs can be traced back to the Cotswolds in England around the 1700s and may have influenced the hedge chair seen in Ireland (see page 18). The first recorded use of the name 'Windsor' is around 1740. The method of making is known as Slab and Stick. Historically there have been several variations in the form, some are high backed, others quite low. There are arm chairs and side chairs, all have the legs set into a plank at angles, in the past they were generally made without stretchers but modern designs tend to include a variety of different shaped stretchers.

above: Ray Walsh at work
far left: Windsor armchair
(black stain)
below (3): Windsor armchair detail

Gabriel Casey

Gabriel Casey's chairs are an expression of the landscape, he uses hawthorn to create strong, 'gnarly' animated pieces that function exceptionally well as chairs. In this wild Irish landscape, the hawthorns grow slowly, their shapes sculpted by the force of relentless westerly gales. The trees twist their faces away from the wind and their roots reach down to grip the earth, they emerge slowly and implacably from the ground. Gabriel's chairs feel as though they are still well-rooted in the rocky soil of County Clare.

His work is typified by the meticulously handmade tenons, shaped with a draw knife and an ingenious sanding drum he designed and made for the purpose.

Gabriel Casey is connected with his chairs from tree to final object, the relationship and collaboration are evident in his designs. They are so personal to him, that you would recognise one his chairs as easily as you would recognise him, anywhere.

Chairs are usually commissioned and Gabriel spends time with the customer working out exact dimensions and style details before starting to make the chair. The seats are woven from white sisal.

**An Geag Cam
(The Crooked Branch)
Cahermakerla
Lisdoonvarna**

Co.Clare
Tel. 00 353 (0)65 7074765
gabrielcasey@eircom.net

left: Gabriel weaving a sisal seat
above: Gabriel using a drawknife
opposite page: hawthorn table with
burr elm top

Thomas Kay

Each one of Thomas Kay's chairs or stools is carved from a single piece of wood.

He uses a chain saw to shape them and, like a sculptor, he liberates the chair from the trunk of a tree. The chainsaw is like a paint brush in his hands, describing gentle curves and creating fine details, that would seem impossible to achieve with such a brutal piece of equipment.

Thomas is both architect and artist, he works from detailed drawings and plans, designing and sculpting in one organic process.

His work is intriguing because it combines a symmetrical form with the wild grain that runs through it. He uses dense-grained hardwoods which grow slowly, combining strength with flexibility.

Thomas works methodically responding to the tree's energy, mindful of the tensions within to reveal the beauty of its grain. His work demonstrates the interaction between mind, tools, and materials. He creates chairs that feel as strong and permanent as the trees they come from, barely separated from the landscape that created them.

Coomkeen
Durrus
Bantry
County Cork

Tel. 00 353 (0)27 61048
thomas@kayartdesign.com
www.kayartdesign.com

above: Thomas at work
left: carved elm foot stool
far left: carved (and coloured)
beech chair

127

Mike Miall

Portaferry
County Down BT22 1NB
Northern Ireland

Tel. 00 44 (0)28 42772418
mikemiall@supanet.com

Mike Miall spent 40 years in the RAF. He had always enjoyed wood turning and when he retired took a course in Welsh Stick chair making. This led him to Windsor chairs and a whole new life as a chair maker.

He has an impressive collection of traditional tools such as travishers for scooping out the seat by hand and rounding planes for use with the lathe. He uses many of the tools in his collection on a daily basis while the others intrigue him — the feel of them and the knowledge of how they were used in the past.

Mike sticks to the traditional method of Windsor chair making. He uses a single elm plank for the seat, with the arm bows made from either straight grained ash which is steam bent or a composite of three pieces of elm. He uses homemade jigs and devices that make it possible to work with only one pair of hands. (The exception being his steam bending when he needs the help of his wife to grasp one end as the two ends are too far apart for one person's stretch.) The resulting chairs are robust, elegant and beautifully finished. They are close to perfect but unlike production-line pieces, they retain character and a handmade feel.

left: Mike working with a travisher
below: Mike shaping a composite arm bow
opposite page: Mike with a Welsh stick chair

Joe Lawler

Architectural Furniture
Donacarney
County Meath

Tel. 00 353 (0) 41 982 7124
www.architectural-furniture.com
joelawler@eircom.net

Joe Lawler comes from a long line of woodworkers. He loves to use locally sourced native hardwoods and has been fortunate in finding some unusual woods on the estates in his area. Joe's chairs are neither traditional post and rail nor slab and stick construction. Their throne-like shapes bear some resemblance to the Sligo/Tuam chair but they are based more on geometry and sculpture.

As with most other Irish chair makers, Joe works on his own in a workshop at home. Most of the tools and equipment he uses are recognisable as wood work fundamentals: planer/thicknesser, band saw, sanders and so on. However, the chairs he produces are a far cry from the conventional designs we would normally expect to see.

Joe has developed a very personal design approach based on sculptural shapes, inspired to some extent by architecture but also influenced by the trees themselves. The quality of craftsmanship is outstanding, the finish beautiful and the use of interesting grain intriguing. His chairs are recognisable wherever you see them, sometimes made from cherry, sycamore or oak, often foraged from the land of local estate owners. Joe was commissioned to make a seat for the offices of the Drogheda Port Company, in Drogheda, County Louth. Entitled the Mariner Chair, this piece beautifully reflects the curves and forms of a boat, whilst retaining perfect functionality as a seat.

above: Joe at work
left: 'That's Right' chair, in Irish canary elm
opposite page: Mariner chair in Irish silver cedar

James Carroll

The Playhouse
Chapel Lane
Glenealy
County Wicklow

Tel. 00 353 (0)404 44849
james@stickman.ie

James Carroll is an artist at heart and sees chairs as functional sculpture. His long training has been in the use of a wide variety of materials. He has made chairs from found objects and recycled materials as well as wood. Carroll's workshop is filled with beautiful timber planks, tree stumps and many works in progress. He collects wood because it is beautiful and inspires him to create.

James appears to work for the sheer joy of the creative process. His influences range from chair makers such as George Nakashima and Daniel Mack to the work of traditional oak-frame house builders and vernacular furniture makers. He is fascinated by the possibilities of working with materials that have been used and discarded, he seeks to give them another life. In a society that scorns second-hand or used items, James sees the value of materials that have proved their worth. 'Hand working green wood is so satisfying ... it is something primal. We've been doing it for thousands of years. It is part of us and I think that is why people respond so favourably to real wood ... now, more than ever, it provides a needed link, it engages us with the physical world.'

above: Old rocker
left: Tyred lounger
opposite page: Megleg chair
following page: Rosa in the woods,
birch and oak chair with cherry seat

Chapter 11

Budding green wood chair makers

11. Budding green wood chair makers

There is at least one chair in all of us
Author

Making a green wood chair affects those around us and may inspire others to make one too. I have been fortunate to teach over 200 students to make all sorts of chairs, stools and tables. Students bring me innovative ideas and open-minded approaches. They arrive at my studio, believing that everything is possible and suggest ways of designing and making that often challenge my approaches and methods. This is a very good thing, it keeps me thinking about what I do and forces me to explain, as much to myself as to them, why I do things in a particular way.

below: Green Wood Chairs
workshop with Buffy
opposite page: removing 'snags'
with whittling knife

Some students' ideas may be off the wall yet I find I change my way of working because of these ideas. The new can always be incorporated and no two chairs go out of my workshop looking exactly the same. I am surprised at how often I say 'no one has ever done that before.'

This aspect of teaching is very exciting as my role becomes that of a facilitator or even a midwife. The student has an idea or vision and I supply the materials, techniques and opportunity (and encouragement) for bringing that chair into existence. I am constantly surprised by the new ways in which a green wood chair can be made.

Some students will only ever make one chair. The three days spent making it will be fondly remembered and every time they use the chair, they will proudly think 'I made this.' Others come in order to learn new skills and make more chairs, sometimes as gifts for family and friends or with the intention of selling chairs. Each time they make a new one, they build up their skills and abilities, developing a style of their own.

*top: Alison in front of eco friendly Green Wood workshop with view of studio
above: Green Wood workshop and studio with Hero and Big Yellow Dog
opposite page: Mike Prankerd with two of his many green wood chair designs*

Paula Bradley with a selection of her own green wood chair designs inspired after completing a three-day course

The personality of the chair maker impacts on the kind of work they do. There are students who strip all the bark off, others who want to use every odd, crooked stick they can find. Some work methodically and with precision, others rush into it, eager and impatient to see how sticks can become a full-sized chair. All have a smile on their face as they work away, seeing the chair take shape under their hands.

People who want to make green wood chairs seem to already understand each other. It is as if we are part of a mysterious brother/sisterhood and although we have never met before, all of us understand the secret mystery of the tree, of whittling, peeling, joining and ultimately creating something functional and beautiful. We revel in the sounds of knife blades scraping, bark fibres tearing, tenons creaking as they twist. We know it and we leave it unsaid because words cannot begin to describe it and might even break the spell.

Appendix

Resources

Coppice Association of Ireland
00 353 87 742 8084 contact Joe Gowran
Courses in woodland management, coppicing etc. Offer advice on sourcing of coppiced material in Ireland, especially hazel.

Crann
www.crann.ie
A voluntary non-profit organisation dedicated to planting trees and protecting Ireland's woodlands. Regular newsletter, 'Re-Leafing Ireland' on tree -related issues.

Coillte
www.coillte.ie
A commercial company operating in the forestry sector. Coillte owns around 7% of Ireland's forests and woodland. There are eleven forest parks and over 150 recreation sites open to the public in Ireland. Arrangements can be made to coppice and prune trees in your area.

Woodkerne Nurseries, Gortnamucklagh, Skibbereen, County Cork
00 353 28 23384 Paul and Jacinta McCormick
www.woodkerne.com
Specialists in native species fruit and nut trees grown from local seed on organic woodland farm. Also offering tree grafting service, orchard design/management, and educational workshops. Will supply coppiced hazel suitable for chair making.

Saul Mossbacher
00 353 61 924914
Supplies Coppiced hazel during winter months from woodlands in County Clare and County Cork. Can advise on sourcing hazel and other coppice woods.

Peter Collins: Blacksmith
Three Chimney House, Mount Shannon, County Clare
00 353 87 6893265
Peter specialises in producing excellent quality green woodwork tools especially draw knives. Will make to commission.

Tools
Suppliers of all kinds of knives. I get my own excellent chip carving knives made by these 2 craftsmen:

Rory Conner
Handcrafted Knives, Ballylickey, Bantry, County Cork
00 353 27 50032
handcraftedknives@eircom.net
handcraftedknives@eircom.net

Pat Mulcahy
Knife craft, Brook Cottage, Seskin, Bantry, West Cork
00 353 87 7606117
www.knifecraft.biz pat@knifecraft.biz

opposite page: hazel dressing chair with upholstered seat in handmade felt by Helen Stringer

Ben Russell
Kealkil, Bantry, West Cork
00 353 27 66133
benr@esatclear.ie
Supplier of Veritas tenoning attachments and other wood carving tools.

Green Wood Chairs Studio
The Wooden House, Rossnagoose, Skibbereen, County Cork
00 353 28 21890
www.greenwoodchairs.com
alison@greenwoodchairs.com
Supplier of Veritas tenoning attachments and all green wood chair making tools/equipment.
1 and 3 day chair making courses

Dick Tools
www.dick.biz
Suppliers of excellent tools. Catalogue includes many hand tools. Draw knives, chip carving knives, sharpening stones, a variety of tenoning attachments for use with brace or cordless drill.

Seat Weaving Supplies
00 44 (0) 1202 895859
www.seatweavingsupplies.co.uk
sales@seatweavingsupplies.co.uk
Suppliers of rush rope, paper rush and various seating materials.

Ashem Crafts
00 44 (0) 1905 640070
www.ashemcrafts.com
Produce many of their own tools as well as Shaker tape for seating, hollow shoulder augers and rounding planes see web site for catalogue and listing.

Vintage Tools

Ray Iles
The Old Tool Store
Whitehaven Farm, Boston Road, Horncastle, Lincolnshire, LN9 6HU
00 44 (0) 1507 525697
www.oldtoolstore.com
Suppliers of old tools and producers of a wide variety of new green wood tools.

Tom Thackray
Tindale Bank Workshop, Haxey, Doncaster, DN1 2NW
00 44 (0) 1427 891063
www.tomthackraywindsorchairs.com
tomthackray@btinternet.com
Supplies his own hand made travishers for scooping out seats also supplies rounding planes. Runs a well established 5 day Windsor chairmaking course for 1 or 2 students at a time.

Living Wood Ltd
Bishops Frome, Worcester, WR6 5AS
00 44 (0) 1531 640005
abbot@livingwood.co.uk
www.living-wood.co.uk
You Tube — Greenwood Workshop
Mike Abbott holds courses from May to September lasting either 3 or 6 days making use of green wood, grown in the Herefordshire woodlands which surround his workshop. The courses are based on the local chairmaking tradition using cleaving brakes, shaving horses and pole-lathes.

www.rodmiller.com
Managers of a variety of estates in Wiltshire and Dorset can supply coppiced hazel for chair making.

To find information on coppices in UK contact:
www.coppice-products.co.uk

Acknowledgements

To Jose with thanks for his patience and understanding of my ideas and for his insightful contributions to the book.

To Jane and Nigel Evans for making me take responsibilty for my work and ensuring that we would produce a worthy book.

To my children Ana, Eddy and Rosa for simply believing that I could do it, when even I was not certain.... and to Clara my niece, for making me realise that I live in the perfect place for writing books.

Thanks also to Ben Russell and Roland Paschhoff, the brilliant photgraphers whose images bring this book to life and to Mike Prankerd for his illustrations, they have proved that a picture's worth a thousand words.

To Lissard Estate, West Cork for their kind permission to use their stunning gardens for a photo shoot and also to Jacinta and Paul McCormick for giving us access to their hazel trees and woodland for a photo shoot.

Art Complex Museum, Duxbury, Massachusettes USA

National Museum of Ireland, Collins Barracks, Benburb Street, Dublin 7

opposite page: hazel side chair
with elm seat

Bibliography

Abbott, Mike *Living Wood* Living Wood Books, Worcester, Great Britain 2002

Adamson, Jeremy *The Furniture of Sam Maloof* Smithsonian American Art Museum, USA 2001

Capra, Fritjof *The Turning Point* Harper Collins, London 1983

Coaldrake, William *The Way of the Carpenter* Weatherhill, New York 1990

Cranz, Galen *The Chair* W W Norton & Co Inc, Date, USA 1998

Day, Christopher *Building With Heart* Green Books, UK 1990

Dodds, Margaret K *Easy to Build Wooden Chairs for Children* Dover Publications, New York 1984

Goldsworthy, Andy *Wood* Viking, Great Britain 1996

Hardy, Thomas *The Woodlanders* Penguin, London 1974

Hill, Jack *Country Woodworker* Mitchell Beazley, Great Britain 1995

Johnson, Kay and Elton Barratt, Olivia and Butcher, Mary *Chair Seating* Dryad Press, London 1990

Kinmonth, Claudia *Irish Country Furniture* Yale University Press, USA 1993

Larusso, Carol Spenard (Editor) *The Green Thoreau* New World Library, USA 1992

Lawrence, D H *The Rainbow* Penguin, London 1915

Mack, Daniel *Making Rustic Furniture* Lark Books, USA 1992

Memory Paterson, Jacqueline *Tree Wisdom* Thorsons, London 1996

opposite page: hazel 'dancing' chair with cherry seat

Nakashima, George *The Soul of a Tree* Kodansha International, USA 1981

Rieman, T and Burks, J *The Complete Book of Shaker Furniture* Abrams, New York 1993

Tabor, Raymond *Traditional Woodland Crafts* Batsford, Great Britain 1994

Tabor, Raymond *The Encyclopedia of Green Woodworking* Eco-Logic books, Great Britain 1990

Other Stobart Davies titles

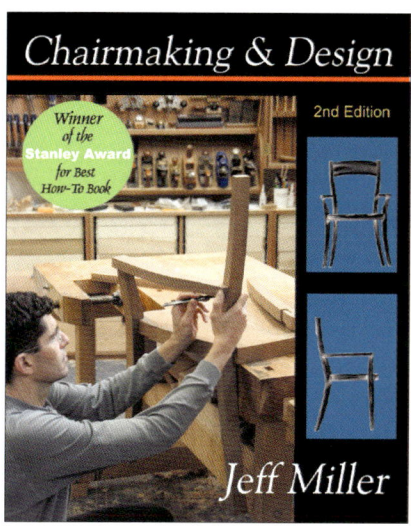

£16.95 SB
ISBN 978-0-85442-155-8
204 x 254 mm 208pp
26 col 111 BW

Chairmaking & Design 2nd Edition
Jeff Miller

An award-winning designer and builder demonstrates the key design elements behind all chairs and provides jig designs for simple construction.

£9.95 SB
ISBN 978-0-85442-083-4
187 x 246 mm 94pp
63 bw 18 line

Welsh Stick Chairs
John Brown

A fascinating glimpse into the history of Welsh stick chairs with a detailed description of the making of a beautiful Welsh armchair, including bending, shaping, and making the legs and sticks for the back.
Includes tributes to the late John Brown.

£24.95 HB
ISBN 978-0-85442-130-5
210 x 297 mm 192pp
228 col 14 bw 16 line

The Wooden Bowl
Robin Wood

The first authoritative account of the history of the wooden bowl. It details evidence of the turners craft dating back 4000 years and looks at the development of lathe technology, as well as the tools and timbers used.

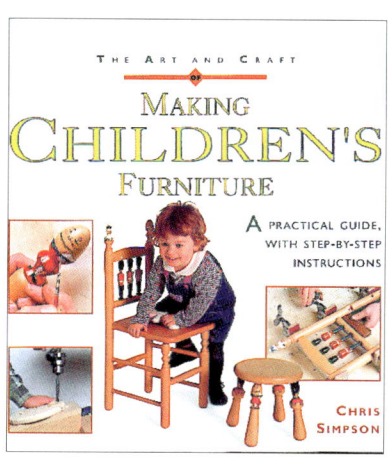

£15.95 HB
ISBN 978-0-85442-064-3
232 x 230 mm 176pp
256 col 109 line

The Art and Craft Of Making Childrens Furniture
Chris Simpson

A comprehensive book for designing and creating original and stylish children's furniture. Includes projects, materials, construction techniques, decoration and safety.

£19.95 HB
ISBN 978-0-85442-008-7
146 x 223 mm 160pp
8 bw 54 line

What Wood is That?
A Manual of Wood Identification
Herbert L Edlin

A unique book containing a fold-out wallet with 40 actual veneer samples. Each wood is described in terms of 14 key characteristics to teach the method of identifying these and other woods. Illustrated.

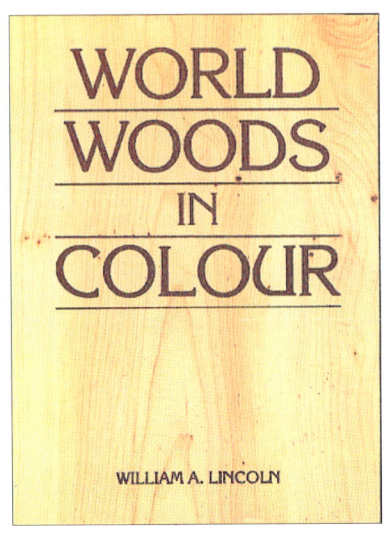

£29.95 HB
ISBN 978-0-85442-028-5
175 x 254 mm
320pp 299 col

World Woods in Colour
William A Lincoln

This authoritative and hugely popular reference book contains almost 300 colour illustrations showing the natural grain and colour of wood, along with data that includes distribution, properties and uses of more than 300 timbers from world-wide sources.

£14.95 SB
ISBN 978-0-85442-145-9
166 x 233 mm 496pp
950+ line

1001 Tips for Woodworkers
Percy Blandford

The tips cover all aspects of woodworking with hand and power tools. There are ways to improve the use of traditional and new handtools, and ways to get the most out of the many hand and stationary power tools available today. Workshops and their equipment are covered, from compact to extensive, improvised and permanent.

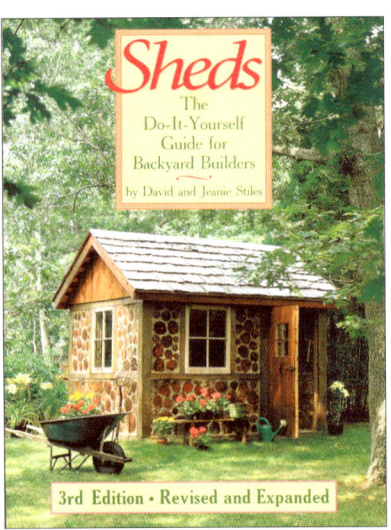

£16.95 SB
ISBN 978-1-55407-224-8
206 x 276 mm 208pp
49 col 208 line

Sheds
The Do-It-Yourself Guide for Backyard Builders
3rd Edition Revised and Expanded
David and Jeanie Stiles

Everything you need to know on building your own purpose-built shed. Includes examples of sheds, design, size, cost, placement, and use. Step-by-step illustrations describe the construction of seven different sheds.

Stobart Davies Ltd

Stobart House, Pontyclerc, Penybanc Road, Ammanford SA18 3HP, UK
Tel: +44 (0) 1269 593100   Fax: +44 (0) 1269 596116
sales@stobartdavies.com   www.stobartdavies.com